HEART AND SOIL
NORTHERN MICHIGAN WINE COUNTRY

CHRIS KASSEL
DESIGN BY JESSE KASSEL

Paperback Edition
First Printing 2014

Copyright © 2014 by Christian Kassel

Published by Rhapsody In Rust Press LLC

ISBN-13: 978-1503370180
ISBN-10: 1503370186

Book & Bottle Club

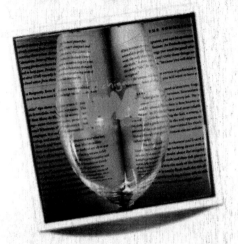

Love to read? Love wine? Us, too!
Join us on select Wednesdays and Thursdays,
7-8 p.m., for MBTB's book club!

For details, join our Facebook group at
facebook.com/groups/bookandbottle or visit
MBTBTasting.com/events

Upcoming Dates

February: "Books You Loved in High Scho
Wed. Feb. 1 @ MBTB Auburn
"To Kill a Mockingbird"
by Harper Lee

Thurs. Feb. 16 @ MBTB Royal Oak
"The Outsiders"
by S.E. Hinton

March: "Family Tales"
Thurs. March 2 @ MBTB Shelby
"Big Fish"
by Daniel Wallace

Thurs. March 16 @ MBTB Royal Oak
"My Grandmother Asked Me
to Tell You She's Sorry"
by Frederik Backman

PREFACE

April 30, 2014: *It's basically May and there's still snow in the vineyards. In fact, there's still snow in the* forecast. *The leaden ice sheet that lingers over Grand Traverse Bay is bizarre; this stretch of water, generally South Pacific turquoise at this time of year, is the color of a blunt object.*

This winter has been the pit-bull that won't let go. Doomsday scenarists in the Leelanau Peninsula are predicting a primary bud failure of 80% for the upcoming growing season, and even the most simpering optimists believe that 40% of 2014's wine harvest may have already been lost. It is largely a varietal-specific phenomenon, with namby pamby cultivars like merlot being the worst off while hybrids and the standby brute, Riesling, will likely fare better.

For the others, it is too early to tell—a lot of them have not yet been put to such a Herculean test of mettle.

One thing upon which everyone agrees is that Northern Michigan wine country is emerging from the worst vine disaster since 1993/1994—a winter so cold that in its wake, the Michigan wine industry essentially had to re-invent itself. Although, by the way, the twin peninsulas of Leelanau and Old Mission did so with oomph: Note that in 1993, hardly any of the current stock of wineries even existed.

If there is a silver lining to this dastardly cloud of horticultural reality, it may simply be that it could have been worse: Our Ohioan rivals wound up on the worse end of the weather stick. Without the meteorological marvel known as 'lake effect', successive days of sub-zero temperatures can kill not only the buds that form on the canes in the fall, but the vines themselves; if that happens, there is little to do but start over. Ironically, both here and south of the border, the season's prodigious snowfall was a blessing, insulating the vines at ground level and keeping the exposed root stock as much as ten degrees warmer than the ambient air.

Remember the old witticism suggesting that 'the first human to eat an oyster must have had some balls'? Same props go to the very first pioneer in the frozen biosphere of Northern Michigan who planted a commercial grape vine. (Bernie Rink, for the record). But a new generation of winemakers keeps on coming and they keep on planting and the late, unlamented Polar Vortex be damned.

There are now 25 wineries on the two peninsulas, each producing a portfolio of uniquely Michigan takes on classic and newfangled varieties. As you might imagine, they are predominantly white wines, and most of them go very well with oysters, thank you very much.

This tome is the collected results of several trips I made to this personality-soaked wine country throughout the 2014 growing season and harvest to assess the whole State of the Ouch and the status of the wine industry's rise from the very chilly ashes of the winter's polar vortex—to vinifera grape vines what Hurricane Katrina was to trailer parks. As always, the character of the wines themselves proved less interesting to me than the characters who produced them, although it is fair to say that I love them both. As such, however, these stories must inevitably come across more as portraits of personalities than reviews of wine.

It does pretend to be an all-inclusive overview of the region, neither as a wine appellation or as a tourist destination. Au contraire, *plenty of fine winemakers with genuine spirit and phenomenal products are admittedly overlooked.*

I will suggest, however, that what follows is a representative slice of Northern Michigan wine country, with the unique and the most interesting stories emphasized. Wine is a fluid tale far more than it is a tale of fluid, and as such, Michigan's pioneers, creating multi-faceted gems at the very edge of viticultural sanity, make remarkable subjects for the telling.

- ***Chris Kassel***, *December 2014*

(Cover photo: Chateau Grand Traverse in October)

TABLE OF CONTENTS

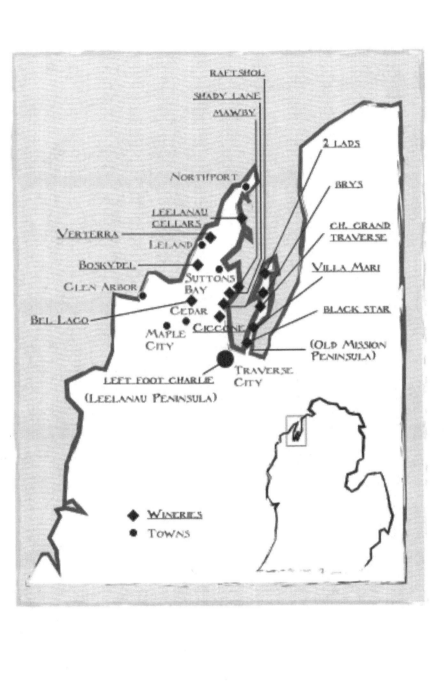

RAFTSHOL

SHADY LANE

MAWBY

2 LADS

BRYS

NORTHPORT

CH. GRAND
TRAVERSE

LEELANAU
CELLARS

VERTERRA

LELAND

VILLA MARI

BOSKYDEL

SUTTONS
BAY

GLEN ARBOR

BLACK STAR

BEL LAGO

CEDAR

CICCONE

(OLD MISSION
PENINSULA)

MAPLE
CITY

TRAVERSE
CITY

LEFT FOOT CHARLIE

(LEELANAU PENINSULA)

◆ WINERIES

● TOWNS

THE APPROACH

On any given evening in late October, the approach to Traverse City is a kaleidoscope of crimson. Severe scarlet slashes rent the skies above the bay; carnal, blood-red fires trickle between troops of trees, down their trunks and across bean fields ablaze with autumn—even the highway that burrows ahead is festooned with splats of deer felled by passing cars.

Magnificent death is all around; leaves, sky, roadkill—bombastic death, technicolor death, but death just the same. When summer dies in Michigan's great North, it goes out with a splurge.

If you head into the city via Highway 37, the explosive palette begins to change around Mason Creek and the deer smears soon become the least ghastly of the sights surrounding you.

Remember the fairy tale where Prince Charming, in order to get to the most beautiful princess in the world, had to fight through a forest of brambles and thorns and mile-high pricker bushes that grew up around the castle where she slept? That's a marvelous metaphor for the outskirts of Traverse City, where the brambles have turned into malnutrition emporiums like Wendy's and Olive Garden with hideous neon signs pushing industrial slop; the thorns are big box monstrosities like Wal-Mart, Target and Sam's Club, while the mile-high prickers are mile-long strip malls clotted with Kohl's and Best Buy and all the zeitgeist dreck you headed north to escape in the first place. It's like the final onslaught of tympanic-membrane-shattering thunder before the sky clears and the air freshens and blue Grand Traverse Bay spreads out in splendor toward the wilderness.

You still have to get through Traverse City, of course, which is—as cities go—not awful. It's the pretty moat around the castle that needs to be tackled before you locate Sleeping Beauty in her secret chamber. It's picturesque and clean, but like any town that survives on (and hence, caters to) visitors, there is a lot of fluff to temper the quaint; plenty of tacky traps into which a tourist can tumble. They're the cherry-candy canal you'll need wade through to get to the prize—Leelanau and Old Mission Peninsulas—and since, barring a boat, you'll have to pass through the heart of it to get to wine country, you might as well stop in at some of the cooler attractions when you do.

The State Theater on Front Street is a landmark that dates from the early Twentieth Century, and it is fair to say that it had its ups and downs from the beginning. For example, it went up in 1916 and burned down seven years later; at the time of the fire, tickets were fifteen cents for adults and a nickel for children. Tempting fate perhaps, the theater—then called The Lyric—reopened on December 20, 1923 with a film called *Hearts Aflame*. George Jessel, performing in *Lucky Boy* sang the first note in the first talkie shown in Traverse City; it coincided with the onset of the Great Depression that produced a whole lot of unlucky boys. The theater burned again in '48 and opened again the following year as The State—the name it would use through the early 1990s when the owners of the Grand Traverse Mall theater complex placed deed restrictions on the landmark which ultimately shut it down. Enter Barry Cole and the State Theatre Group, who bought the building in the hope of converting it to a performing art complex; they partnered with nearby Interlochen Center for the Arts and ultimately, after renovation, the building was donated to The Traverse City Film Festival. Between 'Helping to Save One of America's Few Indigenous Art Forms' (the festival's mission statement), the State is a downtown locus for locals, a comfortable destination for fans of first-run flicks in a non-chain theater surrounded by history, and best of all, affordable popcorn.

Taking your kids to an eskimo museum may not win you the same smiles of gratitude as taking them to Pirate's Cove Adventure Park might, but as soon as they outgrow miniature golf, stop in at the Power Family Inuit Gallery at Northwestern Michigan College, containing what is arguably the most historically complete collection of Inuit art in the

United States. And should they (or any bonafide adult) grow weary of Nanook knick-knacks, the museum is also home to the Milliken Auditorium, a performance venue specializing in jazz and blues.

If your tastes run more to Wolfgang Mozart than Howlin' Wolf, the City Opera House—ground zero for the Traverse Symphony Orchestra—is as architecturally fascinating as it is culturally enriching. 'The Grand Old Lady', as it's known locally, is a historically-accurate Victorian theater listed in the National Registry. The dramatic barrel vault ceiling and magnificent arches emblazoned with *trompe l'oeil* clouds houses ornate frescos with gold leaf accents and has been in continues operation for more than a century.

City Opera House opened in 1891, about fifty years after a sawmill was established on the Boardman River by Chicago entrepreneurs Perry Hannah and Tracy Lay. Oddly, the area had been largely devoid of indigenous people for most of its history; the Ottawa and Chippewa did not settle here permanently until the eighteenth century, and until the first road was built during the Civil War, it was inaccessible by land to most of downstate Michigan.

The railroad followed in 1872—the peninsulas overhead were becoming heavily farmed (mostly potatoes and apples) but it was not the fruit baskets so much as the fruitcakes and basket-cases that turned the town into a metropolis of any significance: The Northern Michigan Asylum was established in 1881 after city founder Perry Hannah petitioned the state to build another psychiatric hospital at Division and 11th in the area now known as Grand Traverse Commons. Bryan Ulbrich's incomparable Left Foot Charlie urban winery is located there. The wretched lead-in joke notwithstanding, the hospital, built in Victorian-Italianate style according to the Kirkbride Plan, was part of a national effort to reform treatment for the mentally ill. 'Beauty as therapy' was a cornerstone of the psychiatric renaissance, and the grounds contained an inmate-run greenhouse that provided fresh flowers year round. The hospital opened in 1885 with 43 residents, and was soon the city's largest employer.

Today, the city's largest employer is tourism, with around a third of all locals jobs tied to that industry via an umbilical cord of commerce. And the wine industry has been instrumental in this reality, especially recently. In 2000, when there were fourteen wineries in Northern Michigan, events essentially ground to a halt after Labor Day; now, Traverse City is busy throughout the year. Even locals who scream and howl about the plethora of festivals—some wine related, some not—that clog up downtown streets, monopolize 'The Open Space' and rain down upon the town the Grinch's reviled *'noise, noise, noise, noise'* don't begrudge the tax coffers their filling.

Most of them, anyway. Last fall, 75-year-old Lou Colombo tried to reserve the entire Open Space (along West Grand Traverse Bay) for the summer of 2014, envisioning a 'Quiet Festival' which would feature the live music of no one and be attended by nobody, thus tossing a wrench into vacation plans of the three million visitors who descend upon the city of 15,000 every year. His protest led City Council to coin the phrase 'festival fatigue' and reduce the maximum number of summer festivals at the Open Space from six to four: The Quiet Festival was not among them, for which we may raise a collective and very loud *'Huzzah!'*

What the wine industry has done for the area more than any other touro-dollar revenue source is extend the season; harvest time is when the wine world springs to life, and the beginning of autumn is, to wine tourism, what the Fourth of July is to cherries. This, in turn, has allowed the auxiliary attractions—restaurants and bars—to operate through the winter. That this could be seen as anything but a plus to Traverse City's population, many of whom I suspect discovered the place long ago via one of the festivals they're now fatigued of, is sort of inexplicable.

So, with the brambles breached and the moat mastered, it is into the palatial twin spires above Traverse City that we head, in search of a Sleeping Beauty or two among the dozens of wineries that sparkle across Leelanau and Old Mission Peninsulas.

We may not lay claim to being Prince Charming, but as long as our kisses are wine-flavored, I am betting that she wakes up anyway.

BERNIE RINK:
THE LAIRD OF LEELANAU

In the beginning, God created Leelanau Peninsula, and very shortly after that, Bernie Rink was born. Today, at 88, you can find him sitting in the half-light at the entrance of Boskydel's tasting room, exactly where a bouncer would sit if Boskydel needed a bouncer. But, with an *Open* sign that easily flips over to *Go Away* and Bernie owning the reputation as someone who doesn't suffer fools gladly, no outside muscle is required. Known locally as 'The Wine Nazi' after Seinfeld's soup-strict character, the tasting room remains a place where only non-fools dare to tread.

Lest Bernie consider me a fool, I thought better of naming this chapter *The Little Librarian Who Could... And Did,* even though it would have been perfectly accurate. But it is not sufficiently deferential, and although Bernie Rink is somewhat self-effacing in a ferocious, confident sort of way—and even though he is, in fact, a little (ex) librarian—the truth of the matter is that in the intervening Biblical years between Leelanau's formation and Bernie's eureka moment in the early 1960s, nobody up here had thought to put a wine grape vine into the ground. Now, it's about *all* anybody thinks about, and so, credit where it's due: Humble schmumble—leave that for the pie. When Mr. Rink sits at his doorway and looks across the expanse of vineyards that festoon this fair finger of frontier farmland, he is truly the monarch of all he surveys.

And in my book, that is worth a boatload of deference, with a little reverence thrown in for good measure. Thus, of course, this—in many ways—becomes a chapter in *his* book.

Bernie Rink came from an Avon, Ohio subsistence farm where his father grew truck (his word) and surfaced from the Depression by selling bootleg wine for three dollars a gallon. Ohio was—and is—an often overlooked wine region; in the years after the Civil War, it produced more wine than any other state in the country. It was mostly forgettable stuff, no question, and Bernie uses the pejorative 'foxy' to describe wines made from the widely-grown Ohioan wine grapes Catawba, Niagara and Delaware while admitting that his father's bootleg barrels were likely at the lower end of that spectrum. But the whole process fascinated him, and with ethanol in his bloodstream—

figuratively more than literally—he went off to his first post-college job as a librarian at Northwestern Michigan College. There, according to his son Jim (an excellent writer who has chronicled much of the human history of Leelanau with wit and detail), Bernie came upon a book on winemaking by Phil Wagner and decided to revive his latent—and now legal—winemaking skills by planting a number of grape cuttings purchased from Wagner's Maryland nursery.

"The first plot was a single test acre; by then I owned sixteen acres in the center of the Peninsula. It was all a wild experiment—no one had ever grown wine grapes up here. I worked with Stanley Howell of Michigan State University—he brought students up here as a field research opportunity."

Those students may have counted themselves among the lucky ones; Rink's five sons, not so much. Taking the whole enterprise very personally, Jim writes in his essay, 'Field Of Dreams in Leelanau County':

'I first realized that my father was serious about growing grapes when he announced his intention to raze our modest, but popular baseball diamond in favor of a nursery. My brothers and I created that ball park, hacking it out from a fallow field with a regular push-type lawnmower. We even built a substantial chicken-wire backstop to halt the progress of an errant pitch.

'In a rude reversal of the magical 'Field of Dreams' scenario, Bernie Rink told us the diamond would have to go, replaced by a crop that no one in those parts had ever heard of: Wine grapes.'

To add insult to injury, Jim suspects that Bernie saw the vineyard as an ideal way to keep the boys occupied. He goes on to lament:

'As economic assets, we were expected to chop weeds in the sweltering heat of mid-summer and pick grapes in the stinging sleet of late fall. Not to mention pruning in knee-deep snow in the winter and sorting out the good wood, which would be plunged into our new-found nursery in the spring to repeat the endless, monotonous cycle.

"But it was fun. We used to make up lively little songs about the vineyard to the tune of 'Tah, Rah, Rah, Boom-de-ay':

> *"We work at Boskydel,*
>
> *the closest thing to hell.*
>
> *We're never treated well,*
>
> *at Slave Camp Boskydel."*

JIM RINK

As it happens, Jim and his brother Andy Rink are still at work at Slave Camp Boskydel. While Bernie holds court in his seat by the doorway, they're the ones behind the tasting-room counter, quality control and the day-to-day winemaking grind; it's a regular three Rink circus.

According to Jim, the vineyard test lasted seven years, and during that time, score was kept, with points going to the varieties that survived the frosty finger relatively unscathed, meaning, were resistance to disease and winter-kill while still producing commercial quantities of grapes that could make commercially sellable wine. Meanwhile, Bernie's buddy, retired chemistry professor Bob Herbst, had a similar experiment going on the eastern shore of the peninsula and over the years, they compared notes. In the end, Rink settled on Soleil Blanc, Vignoles, Seyval, Aurore, Cascade Noir and De Chaunac—varietals that produced the dry, French-style wines that he was after without actually being French grapes. Chardonnay and Pinot Noir gave Bernie their best shot, but didn't make the final cut.

As for Riesling, the *vinifera* that most experts believed showed promise in Leelanau, Bernie says, "I planted it in what turned out to be a natural wildlife corridor between a couple of swamps. In short, the deer ate all my Riesling. That took care of that."

Those were the early Seventies; now, in the middle teens of a new century, Rink remains reliant on hybrid grapes; especially De Chaunac. Among his current labels, there's nary a *vinifera* to be found—and none needed. As the liner notes note, some obscurely-named publication called the *Baxevanis American Wine Review* considers Boskydel De Chaunac the best wine of its kind in the United States.

Speaking of obscure names, Bernie Rink speaks with fond nostalgia about the late Professor Al Bungart, to whom he refers as 'a one-suspender farmer and professor; both my mentor and my friend.' Al wrote a Tolkien-esque poem called *'The Elves of Bosky Dingle'*, which was never officially published, but reaches the hoi polloi via the Boskydel (edited into a bite-sized word by bookworm Bernie) label, depicting a couple of elves—not monks as has been suggested—filching wine from a vat. Although to Bernie's amusement someone suggested that 'bosky' is a synonym for 'drunk', it's more likely a derivation of the Middle English *bosk*, from Anglo-Latin *bosca* for 'firewood'. Without debate, however, the dingle in the jingle is a dell.

Outside the battered barn that serves as the wine-talk locus at Boskydel sits a tractor, a trash can and either a snow shovel or a chair for Bernie, depending on the season. Inside is a rustic, lived-in tasting room heated with a wood stove and hung with mostly obscure and often private-joke photographs. It's been described as 'primitive' and 'off-putting', but since it only has a capacity of eight, neither descriptor matters to those wine people in search of local lore and all-go, no-show legend and not just another tour bus whistle stop.

Jim and Andy, who have not yet achieved curmudgeon status, seem more eager to chat and swap tales than oversell the wine. And gratefully so: At under twelve dollars a bottle, the used-car sales approach is neither appropriate nor necessary.

In short, this is the sort of rinky-dink roadside attraction that gives the multi-million dollar-hoopla hoop vineyard being erected on Old Mission Peninsula a run for my money.

"We've had customers loyal for thirty-eight years," says Jim. "We sell everything we make, so we don't worry much about judges or competitions. We love our repeat customers, but one newer group with which we've had a lot of success are Millennials; they don't seem to have as many preconceptions about wine; they don't have the brand loyalty of their parents, but they also don't come in demanding Pinot or Riesling..."

What most of them come in to find is a set of varietals they've never even heard of let alone tried—an introductory course to the unique Land of Hybridia; wines with an individual backstory.

You either like this kind of experience or you don't. I'm a 'do'.

Soleil Blanc means 'white sun'; a bit more poetic than its former name, Seibel 10.868, but that hasn't made the grape more vineyard-popular. In fact, I can't find another winery that produces it. Rink's Soleil statement is bright and brisk with a pineapple-scented bouquet, a tropical palate and a sharp, acidic conclusion.

Vignoles is among the most successful hybrid in Michigan; vinified dry like Boskydel's it produces a soft, supple wine resplendent with notes of green apple and undertones of peach. Rink's 2012 Vignoles is tinged with an unexpected touch of clove and a stylish citrus finish.

Seyval Blanc is a viticulture balancing act; it ripens early and can fight off the most inclement winter weather, but is susceptible to the twin mildews, powdery and down, while producing large clusters that can rot (nobly or otherwise) if not picked at peak ripeness. When it is, the result is as demonstrated in Boskydel's 2013—a round, Chenin-like profile with melon and grapefruit on the nose and a creamy apple mid-palate. As with all of Bernie's wines, there is a finish that's shivery-crisp with acidity.

Boskydel's go-to red wine grape is De Chaunac; the winery produces a full-bore chocolate-cherry version that is firm on the palate and filled with tart boysenberry flavors and very light oak notes. The rosé is an equal palate-pleaser, with bright raspberry and watermelon in the nose and a sweetness that the Rinks emphasize comes only from Michigan-grown beet sugar. Talk about locavoracity.

In fact, so insular is Bernie Rink that when I asked him about Villa Mari's above-mentioned hoop vineyard being erected a few miles away on Old Mission, he shook his head; he hadn't heard of it.

"I never leave the county," he maintains with a shrug. "Ever since they put up the third traffic light on Division, even Traverse City is too damn much for me."

Which works out fine for the rest of us. Primogeniture being what it is and two Rink brothers manning the bottle stations, there is no doubt that Bernie Rink's scepter will pass into worthy and deserving hands— hands that rose from the Rink ranks of indentured servants at Slave Camp Boskydel and now run the plantation.

Until the final curtain, the sight of Bernie in his chair by the door— autumn light filtering in from the doorway, rows of vines tumbling down toward the bay—remains one of the transient glories of Leelanau Peninsula.

LARRY MAWBY:
'FEEL MY PACNE'

Saying that Larry Mawby has a sparkle in his eye may be metaphorical, but the one in his glass isn't.

Lately, Michigan's premier producer of sparkling wine has been getting some pretty hearty recommendations from beyond the narrow confines of Northern Michigan: In 2013, for example, *Vineyard and Winery Management* named him one the twenty most admired wine industry people in North America—right up there with Kevin Zraly, Jerry Lohr and Randall 'Don't Call Me A Cracker' Grahm, and in his 2006 book *The Great Wines of America: The Top Forty Vintners, Vineyards, and Vintages,* Paul Lukacs listed only two sparkling wines—one of them, Mawby's 'Talismon'. Although Larry has been producing bubbly wines exclusively since 2003, his star seems to be rising pretty steadily of late—and sparkling in the enological heavens while it does.

So I jumped at the chance when Larry offered to 'show me where the magic happens.'

Now, when a business-type uses that particularly loathsome catchphrase, you can usually count on seeing something pretty mundane. But the massive press in front of Larry's hidden 4th Street Winery, squirreled away among white pines and maples, is impressive. Draped in a huge gray tarp, it looks like Mawby is showing me his secret menagerie and this is the elephant.

But if it's a zoo, it's a *parc zoologique*, since most of the pets are French. Inside, there's an elevated gyropalette from Epernay—a huge cage that gyrates bottles through a steadily increasing set of angles, causing causes the yeast sediment to slowly settle into the neck. This is in advance of *dégorgement*, for which he also has a machine from Champagne. And he uses something else French to add the *dosage*—a bit of sugar water to kick start the second fermentation (the one that leads to bubbles), and there's a corker and hooder singing, *'Allons enfants de la Patrie'* as well, and thick-walled bottles from Reims. In fact, the only thing he can't import from Champagne is their name, but that's cool: He's got a sparkling wine called 'Sex', and that pretty much deconstructs the subject to its most essential element anyway, doesn't it?

And with 'Sex' on the label, you really don't need the additional aphrodisiac of an *appellation d'origine*.

So, if Larry can distill the drink down to its basics in a single word, then maybe I can use a couple more to describe the process by which juice from generally under-ripe wine grapes is transformed into the beverage about which Dom Perignon was said to exclaim, *"I am drinking the stars..."*

The trio of grapes responsible for most correctly-labeled Champagne— wines from the historic French province of Champagne that have undergone secondary fermentation in the bottle—are Pinot Noir, Chardonnay and, to a punier extent, Pinot Meunier. Champagne producers often (but not always) blend all three to create a unique cuvée, assemblage or 'house style'. Champagne grapes are among the earliest harvested, always by hand and over about a three-week period, primarily to preserve the fruit's natural acidity and the curious delicacies and nuances of flavor in slightly under-ripe grapes. Chaptalization—the addition of sugar to boost alcohol—is not only permitted in Champagne, but sometimes necessary. The region is near the northern border of where viticulture is even possible, and ripening is always an iffy proposal.

Adding sugar to under-ripe grapes to pump the proofage is not to be confused with *dosage*—a critical step which occurs later in the game in order to push the wine's final sweetness to one of the several levels required in the classifications of less-than-bone-dry Champagne.

But, I'm getting ahead of myself. Before *dosage* sugar is added, *triage* sugar, along with yeast and nutrients, is dissolved in the fermented *cuvée*, and the concoction is transferred into heavy bottles and sealed with a cap. Secondary fermentation—the critical step that distinguishes *méthode champenoise* from other methods of imparting bubbles to wine—occurs inside the bottle. Once this has happened, and the yeast cells die, they collect at the bottom and add complexity and those characteristic 'doughy' flavors to the wine.

But a clot of sediment is a no-no in sparkling wines, of course, and in order to remove it, a complicated, time-consuming process known as 'riddling' must occur. *Le Remuage* in French, the bottles are carefully inverted in progressive steps, often by hand, and the yeast sludge slowly moves up the neck where it finally settles against the crown cap. Next, during disgorging (*dégorgement* in French), a small amount of wine containing the plug of lees is frozen and removed. That's when the *dosage* mentioned earlier is added, along with sulphur dioxide to prevent oxidation. The amount of sugar added depends on the winemakers end-game of making *ultra brut* (very dry) up to *doux* (sweet). The middle-ground, called *brut*, is by far the most common.

The wine is then stoppered with a special cork and wired shut against the considerable pressures that have built up during the second fermentation.

The winemaker may then choose to further age the wine so that the biochemistry of the dosage sugar develops, or it may be released at once.

That overview should give you an idea of the labor intensity of making sparkling wine the *méthode champenoise* way, which to those new waves of 'non-interventionalist' winemakers must look like a Wall Street trading pit looks to an agoraphobic.

And it ain't the cheapest way to make wine, either. On Larry Mawby's first shopping excursion to Europe in 2000, which he spent haunting winemaker garage sales, he dropped eighty grand on fancy Tschampagne tschotchkes. On his second trip, he dropped another eighty, and although it is fair to suggest that he suffers sticker shock to this day, the twin spending sprees put him in the best position imaginable to lead Leelanau into in a future he envisioned as frothy with bubbles and sparkles and *lutte raisonnée*.

"We're farther south than Burgundy—farther south than Champagne, which means that during the summer, our days are shorter. But we get more sunshine than they do—Champagne is even cloudier than Burgundy, and for the most part, we get more hours of sun than either one; almost as much as Bordeaux. That allows us, even with shorter days, to bring our grapes to the ideal fruit parameters for sparkling wine, even in cooler vintages. I made my first sparkling wine in 1984, and twelve years later, in '96, concluded that if that's what I wanted to excel at, that's what I should be producing exclusively."

Purchasing the equipment to do it not only exclusively, but correctly, was a canny commercial move—and time has proven this out. The likelihood that any other Grand Traverse winemaker would put as much initiative into bubbles was slim, and Mawby set up operations so that he could custom-sparkle wines for other locals, who may like to have *mousse* in their medley, but have neither the space nor the cash to do it themselves. Currently, around twenty wineries use his services to put sparkle in their portfolio. Professional courtesy prevents Larry from naming names, of course—and in any case, the list of those Grand Traverse sparkling wines that *don't* use his know-how is a quicker study and can be counted on a single, yeast spackled hand.

One of the reasons for the secrecy centers on the quiet truth that nearly every wine savvy person already knows: Most sparkling wine is made in the cheaper, technically result-equitable bulk method—or, because 'bulk' sounds so Wal-Mart, *Charmat*. Named for Saint-Pourçain-sur-Sioule vine grower Eugène Charmat who, a century ago, discovered that wine could undergo the secondary fermentation in bulk, inside a tank, and then be bottled under pressure, it is the method used exclusively to produce Prosecco and Asti Spumante. The relative inexpensiveness of *Charmat* production is one of the reason why these wines are available at gas stations and party stores, while Veuve Cliquot—and L. Mawby 'Talismon'—are not.

Despite the fact that many perfectly acceptable bubblies are made using *Charmat*, and plenty among them are Larry Mawby's, there is an inevitable association of bulk production with bulky wines. For one thing, the bubbles tend to be larger, which isn't a problem until someone like Don Ho tells you it's a problem, and the flavors can be less subtle or refined as a result of limited contact with the lees. But of equal importance, perhaps, is that without the mysterious and arcane skill set of *méthode champenoise* cellarman, some of the magic of sparkling wine is tarnished. And anything that takes away from that mystique, rightly or wrongly, is perceived to be an imperfection.

§

The path that took Larry from the apple groves of Grand Rapids to the vineyards of Leelanau was fairly direct—he knew from an early age that his destiny did not lie with Honeycrisps and Jonagolds, but among *vitis vinifera* and the hybrids—Vignoles especially—which can produce phenomenal results in Northern Michigan. His father Edwin owned a cherry orchard near Sutton's Bay, and that's where Larry spent his formative summers until the age of thirteen, when Edwin moved the clan up there permanently. After college, Larry did a rite-of-passage hitchhiking tour of Europe where he fell in love with Burgundy's winemaking, and upon his return, he planted a small vineyard on one of the family sites, relying on the hybrid varieties that were once thought to be the only wine grapes capable of surviving the noxious northern wintertime—Marechal Foch, Cascade, Chelois, De Chaunac—the usual, un-Burgundian suspects.

But this was 1973, when growing wine grapes of any variety was considered sort of loopy on the Leelanau Peninsula, where cherries were king and strawberries were queen and the highest level of vino sophistication that most Americans aspired to was learning to pronounce 'Mateus'. Two years later, egged on by Leelanau vine pioneer Bernie Rink, he became convinced that vineyards were not only possible on the peninsula, but had a tremendous untapped potential.

So he bought his own plot of grapeland.

Armed with a three-day winemaking degree from UC Davis (that is not a typo), he released his first wine in 1979.

"It was the ultimate blend," he recalls, "in that it contained every grape I grew. It was called 'Picnic Rosé'."

Yes, if ever there is a name that screams 'Don't take me seriously', 'Picnic Rosé' would be it. And that might have been it considering that he took home State Fair bronze for an apple wine that same year, and trust me, winning a bronze medal at a State Fair is not widely considered to be an auspicious winemaking beginning.

But he hung in there, as dedicated men and women are wont to do. He had a ready outlet for whatever he could concoct—the family farm market, on M22 near Traverse City. To their credit, the Mawbys only sold *local* wine, which, prior to Larry's leap into winemaking, pretty much restricted them to Leelanau Wine Cellars, Chateau Grand Traverse and Bernie Rink's Boskydel Vineyard. By the early 1980s, he was up to a thousand cases annually and was finding unheard-of success with early plantings of Chardonnay. In fact, in 1984 he was vindicated in the puny bronze ignominy by winning State Fair gold with his 1983 Chardonnay.

From there, he was out of the gate and on a bullet train that would ultimately take him to The White House: In 2000, Mawby was asked to provide sparkling wines for a special event to honor George H. Bush's inauguration, and three years later, he'd relinquished the still wine game altogether.

Such specialization has permitted him to start a second label, M. Lawrence, featuring a series of less-expensive wines made using *Charmat*, which he prefers to call *'cuvée close'*, and after all, what's in a label name? One such label name being 'Michigan', since he is content to purchase quality grapes—and even quality grape juice—from anywhere on earth to make these wines.

Mawby's wine degree may only have taken him three days, but his English degree took him considerably longer. As a result, he's among the most literary of Michigan's winemakers, with poetry on his labels (some grapey groaners, granted; like 'freeing time's bouquet' and 'our tongue lies wrapped in mystery') but his regular contributions to *Michigan Wine Country* are gems.

Still, when I pressed him to come up with a Champagne quote to close the chapter, he opted again for a French import rather than one from the cellar of his cerebellum: Lily (of Bollinger Champagne) Bollinger's immortal commentary on when to bask in bubbly:

"I only drink Champagne when I'm happy, and when I'm sad. Sometimes I drink it when I'm alone. When I have company, I consider it obligatory. I trifle with it if I am not hungry, and drink it when I am. Otherwise I never touch it—unless I'm thirsty."

BRYAN ULBRICH:
PUTTING HIS LEFT FOOT FORWARD

Sitting outdoors on one of those quintessential Traverse City summer afternoons that are chilly and hot simultaneously, Bryan Ulbrich pours a glass of something special.

At least, he maintains that it will be special; the vines are young and this is the first vintage ever bottled—the grower planted a single acre and he only ended up with 35 cases.

The wine is as much an oddball in Grand Traverse wine country as Bryan Ulbrich is an icon and Left Foot Charley a landmark: Chenin Blanc.

Chenin Blanc, often called *'Steen'* in South Africa and *'Pineau de la Loire'* in the Loire—two regions responsible for the most alluring incarnations of the variety—is a high-acid grape as suitable for a sparkle as it is for dessert wine: *Sélection de Grains Nobles* from the Loire's Coteaux du Layon are potent, honeyed versions of the latter.

South Africa produces twice the amount of Chenin that France does; in fact, with more than 20% of all their vineland planted to this varietal, they make more than anyone in the world, although the bulk (no pun) is monumentally forgettable. Whereas it has a unique glossary of flavors, showing notes of lime, green apple and especially, an odd overtone of garden shrubbery—what the South Africans call *'fynbos'*— it tends to be somewhat neutral and flat-tasting without a lot of terroir expression. In cooler vintages, it verges on undrinkably acidic, and not only that, the buds tend to break very early in the season.

So why Chenin here in the Great White North and why now? Ulbrich quickly passes the buck:

"The grower insisted, that's why. It was a project he believed in. The first planting failed, and the plants refused to shut down; they were still green in November. Next year, we had better luck, and that's the vintage you're tasting."

Bryan Ulbrich has a habit of trusting his growers, which is one of the reasons he's a Northern Michigan winemakers that I trust implicitly in return. Over the many years that I've been sampling his stock, I can say without question that he rarely fails on delivery.

His youthful, alluring Chenin was no exception. Wines made from first harvests can be mono-dimensional, based in part on root depth, but the aromatics here were bright and strikingly layered, with peach, green plum, guava and—in nascent form—the herbal crunch of late summer that so distinguishes this grape in a wine glass. As vines age, they tend to 'wise up', delving deeper for nuance flavors through various soil strata, and I have no doubt that this is a rising star in the Ulbrich portfolio.

Same with Sauvignon Blanc—another cultivar that doesn't get much airplay across Northern Michigan wine country. In fact, he's been using fruit from Antrim County, the northeastern corner of the region covered here. Antrim soils tend to be denser than the twin peninsulas to the left, with more clay; silt abounds, and there has been little erosion since glacial times. It is, in fact, potato country: A 1928 survey claimed, 'About 33% of the county is swampy or always wet'—an admonition to plant wine grapes somewhere in the other 67%.

And, despite a geological persona that is the polar opposite of the gravelly, well-drained banks of the Garonne in Bordeaux, Ulbrich has found a number of elevated pockets in Antrim with correct sun exposures where the 'green monster'—excessively grassy, super-acidic sauvignon or its counterpart, over-ripe soapiness in the wine—can be fought with success.

Antrim County is part of Bryan Ulbrich's success story—he sees it as an oasis of growth with plenty of potential. Land prices are cheaper and the county is huge; it's where he sees a lot of his future grape harvests originating... grown, as always, by someone else.

"We accepted early that we would not be 'landed' people," he says, tipping a glass of the selfsame sauvignon blanc, where savory tropical pineapple and pink grapefruit surfaces above the fresh hay scents. "I'm not claiming to be an artist, but I am certainly not the world's greatest businessman either. Owning vineyard acres has not been part of the plan."

This allows him to utilize the marketing hook 'Urban Winery'—Left Foot Charley is located in the heart of bustling Traverse City, inside, as it happens, a former mental asylum. I have it on good authority that there is no correlation between that fact and the relative insanity of his 2004 decision to go into winemaking.

That story began when Ulbrich was convinced to postpone a vacation and rescue a local vineyard that had fallen into hard horticultural habits thanks to a new owner who had about as much business growing wine grapes as The Hillside Strangler has dating my daughter. Apparently, vital things like canopy management had been neglected and powdery mildew was threatening the harvest, and even with his best efforts, Bryan was only able to salvage a small crop of Riesling.

That led to a life-changing moment which is best elucidated by plagiarizing his website:

'Throughout Northern Michigan there are numerous small vineyards owned and farmed by individuals who do not have wineries. The grapes were often sent to giant blends. Many of these viticulturists are excellent farmers and deserve to see their work turned into wine.'

Turning their work into wine has been the divine mission of Ulbrich ever since. Setting up shop in the old loony bin—the last Kirkbride Building in Michigan, listed on the National Register of Historic Places in 1978—he partnered with eighteen local growers, each representing a specific terroir, philosophy and varietal repertoire. He produces around fifteen thousand cases of wine annually, which makes him larger than most 'boutique' wineries, but he's held to the boutique mindset by fermenting in 300 gallons lots—from grapes that likewise come from small, fiercely manicured plots of vineland.

For example, take his 'Tale Feather Vineyard' Pinot Gris, 2012; perhaps the nicest manifestation of this intense and interesting variety yet produced in Leelanau.

In Michigan, Pinot Gris has been an experiment in progress since it was first installed by Leelanau's Larry Mawby in 1981 after Myron Redford of Oregon's Amity vineyard sent him cuttings; those vines, now three decades into it, are still producing. But Larry never intended Pinot Gris to be a stand-alone variety, and notes that its contribution to his salubrious, celebrious sparkling wines offered a distinct 'roundness' of flavor that balances the Pinot Noir and Chardonnay. Even now, most Michigan growers with acres to Pinot Gris dabble rather than devote.

"I was impressed that Theresa and Gary decided to plant this somewhat exotic grape," says Bryan, speaking of his Old Mission growers, the Wilsons. "Plenty of farmers would have gone another way and planted a less unfamiliar grape that might have had more face recognition, but would not have achieved greatness."

The west slope of 'Tale Feathers Vineyard'—(which is indeed the correct spelling; I asked) is on an elevated hill overlooking Power Island. The sandy, loamy, two-acre site winds up being ideal Gris ground with a cool bay breeze to sharpen the acids while judicious leaf manipulations draw in enough sunshine to sweeten the pot. In the 2012, it shows a big, sweet nose of honey, melon, baked pear and lemon and delivers equal fullness and fruit across the palate, adding mango to the mélange, finishing with a clarity of Pinot Gris expressiveness.

A 9-iron drive from Tale Feathers Vineyard is Werner and Margrit Keuhnis' 'Island View Vineyard', on the eastern side of the same hill.

The couple is Swiss, and according to Ulbrich, "The vineyard looks Swiss, too, by which I mean, it's perfect."

To which a true *Käser* would reply, 'Not perfect yet...'"

This is where Ulbrich sources Gris' blonder sister grape, Pinot Blanc. Island View (same island; Power) Vineyard covers an acre, and by the time Werner took charge in 2000, it had been through several non-Swiss hands who'd left it in dire need of some TLC. Werner took note of each vine's wish list and hand delivered the prescription: The vineyard is dry-farmed and has not seen a grain of synthetic fertilizer since his tenure began.

Keuhnis is from Bryan's school of canopy management, which is to say that the leaves must be pruned so that sufficient sunshine is allowed to reach the clusters; without it, sugars are not able to develop to optimum. The vineyard faces inland, and is blessed with a thick layer of nutrient-rich, water-retaining loam. The resulting Pinot Blanc (from vintage 2012) is dry and medium-bodied; it exhibits well-defined pinot blanc aromatics of lightly-toasted almond, green apple and quince, nice, moderate mid-palate with a bit of peach and lychee. The acid did not appear to be exactly where it should be, and Bryan confirmed that due to warm weather and fermentation that stopped early, the titrable acid in the final wine was a little low compared to residual sugar.

Still, Bryan's overall fermentation technique is pretty straightforward: He does not fine with agents or use yeast strains that produce a lot of esters. The result in most of his end product, and Pinot Blanc especially, is a non-manipulated wine that reflect what the vintage (as well as the grape) has to offer without being shoved into a costume.

Riesling is the *vinifera* grape grown most aggressively in Northern Michigan, and it's the variety with which which Ulbrich has the most leeway, both in terms of style and grower.

As it is in Germany, Riesling has been considered the lynchpin of the Michigan *vitis vinifera* industry, owing in part to the similarity in climate, but perhaps as much to the simple, sugary Rieslings that were the mainstay wines of a lot of early Michigan wine drinkers with German roots and plebian tastes.

Where the Germans rely on steeply sloped river banks to achieve maximum ripeness, Michigan has hillsides and Grand Traverse Bay. In both locations, grade and water allow grapes to flourish in a climate where they'd otherwise perish during the first January deep-freeze. That said, most Michigan Rieslings (and indeed, Rieslings from anywhere in the United States) have generally paled in comparison to the great German estates of, for example, Rüdesheimer, Johannisberg and Winkel.

Of course, it's a misconception to suppose that all German Riesling is styled like the wines of Rheingau—big, concentrated, long-palate wines that brim with apricot, guava and spiciness. Whereas wines from Lake Michigan Shore, further south, can at least lay claim to a version of a climate that can snag these tasting notes, Northern Michigan cannot. So, Bryan Ulbrich wisely takes his cue not from nonpareil Schloss Vollrads, Kloster Eberbach, Schloss Johannisberg and Künstler, but from the crisper, elegant and often more perfumed wines of the chillier German wine region, the Mosel.

Seventh Hill Farm is in Old Mission's far north, probably beyond the range of the fat ripening and long hang-time that Rheingau Riesling enjoys. Tom and Linda Scheuerman work the five acre site, formerly a cherry orchard, where a southern face creates a solar array ideal for making grape sugar while it can. Soils are gravelly and sandy, equaling drainage—one of Riesling's requisite contract riders. And Bryan's 2012 riesling exploits such canny care and clever conception to the max: It is beautifully crafted, light and lovely with damp stone and key lime scents on the nose; a precisely focused palate showing a core of minerality sprinkled with crisp citrus, pine, green apple and that unmistakable Riesling signet, *goût petrol*.

Currently, Left Foot Charley has a trio of Rieslings on release; beside the aforementioned, Bryan offers a 2013 late harvest version called 'Missing Spire' (named for the architectural feature atop the asylum that disappeared along with the inmates) and comes in at a respectable 3.24 g/L residual sugar. Also, he has begun to produce a lively wine from the youngest block of Riesling vines from Seventh Hill Farm on Old Mission Peninsula; this one is called 'Prose' for reasons I don't entirely grasp, because it is poetry in a glass.

All of these selections show Bryan Ulbrich's golden touch with golden wines; a most bearable lightness of being.

Charlie Edson Rings My Bel

Among Leelanau's unique boutiques, Bel Lago is positioned right out of the chute.

For one thing, it is not in the mainstream 'loop' of money-shot, photo-op, rich man's wineries up and down the coast. For another, it doesn't even seem to be in wine country. All the farms on the way in are planted to corn or hay—a few scraggly apple trees, many left to the wild, are the only fruit to be found; the buildings along Lake Shore between Schomberg and Kabot are not slick tasting rooms, but ramshackle, imploding barns with vintage Fords on cinder blocks out front. Along the fifteen minute drive from Cedar you'll find the kind of old school agricultural spreads that made Oliver Wendell Douglas cream his Ralph Lauren overalls, and by the time you see the first grape vine, you're already in Bel Lago's driveway.

There, leaving your vehicle, you may be greeted by Moses, who is not on premise to part the red sea of Pinot Noir nor to fetch the Ten Commandments of Tasting Room Etiquette, but to play catch. He's Charlie Edson's boxer and either has a Frisbee permanently wedged between his teeth or Charlie has fitted him with a Ubangi lip disc. In any case, the dog will trail behind you and nudge you while John Hall pours you a flight of Bel Lago's finest; Moses doesn't know from tasting wines, but fortunately, John, manning the tasting room, does.

The Bel Lago line-up contains the familiar, the fantastic and the phantasmagorical, including clones and grape varieties that even wine pros have to rack their brains to recall and classify.

Among these, Charlie Edson's most snazzy success is Auxerrois, a grape which even in its native France is prone to certain colloquial confusions. In Alsace, it is treated as a blending grape for Crémant and is so often a component of Pinot Blanc that the name 'Auxerrois' may be used interchangeably in the vineyards. Auxerrois is a cousin to Chardonnay, part of the direct Gouais Blanc and Pinot Noir ancestry, but that doesn't stop Cahors *vignerons* from referring to Malbec as Auxerrois, those in Languedoc-Roussillon for doing the same thing with Valdiguié nor those in France's Moselle (who themselves seem to have pilfered a patronym from Germany) from calling Auxerrois 'Chardonnay'.

It's almost like you need a doctorate in vinology to figure this grape out.

Enter Charlie Edson, Ph.D.

It's one thing to want to be a farmer—all that *land spreadin' out so far and wide, keep Manhattan just gimme that countryside* jazz—it's quite another to pursue an advanced degree in it. Farmer John, Ph.D has a peculiar ring, right? Nonetheless, Charlie Edson, who grew up near Muskegon (where an interest in agriculture is considered normal but an academic obsession with it less so) followed his heart to the soil via the lauded MSU program under the tutelage of G. Stanley Howell—the professor emeritus who has figured largely in the development of Northern Michigan viticulture. From there, Edson signed on as a research tech with Missouri State's viticultural program, spending the next four years at another MSU, but always with his eyes on the Leelanau skies.

"I determined by age eighteen that Leelanau was where I wanted to live, so in Missouri, I saved up vacation days and spent every harvest here. I had a hobby acre planted with various experiments—including the first Dijon clones planted in Leelanau."

In 1987, along with his wife Amy Iezzoni and Amy's folks Domenic and Ruth, he established Bel Lago Vineyards—the *lago* being Lake Leelanau and the *bel* being the view. As a winemaker, Charlie's view is equally *bel:* Long hang-times equal ripe flavors, and the key is learning to deal with the potential downside.

"A lot of wine growers up here pick early to avoid rain, but I am willing to take that risk. Pick early, you've capped the ripeness. If I leave the clusters on the vine and it rains, it takes a few days for the plant to metabolize the water. If the rain doesn't stop, I lose, but I have to say, I have been rewarded more times than not."

And the resulting wines display a broader range of flavors than might otherwise be expected, for reasons that don't require a doctorate to understand. Extending grape ripeness is—no pun—a flavor of the month in viticulture across the globe, but in areas where the harvest season is generally hot and dry, excessive sugar accumulation (often at the expense of pH) can produce wines with aggressive alcohols-by-volume, diluted acids and a somewhat jammy taste profile. They also tend to be rewarded at competitions by judges who have embraced, and in certain cases created, the 'hang-time wine' phenomenon.

But that does not necessarily hold true in Northern Michigan, where grapes often struggle to hit the minimum concentration of sugar needed to produce table wine; chaptalization—the addition of processed sugar to boost must sweetness and corollary alcohol levels—is not only allowed by Michigan regulation, but in dicey vintages it is often required. The standardized Brix scale used to measure the sugar content in grapes before fermentation finds that most table wine is harvested between 19 and 25 °Bx, corresponding to ABVs between 10.8% and 15.1%. Much above 25 °Bx, without specially engineered yeast strains, the concentration of ethanol begins to kill off yeast cells before they have fermented the must to dryness. Not only that, but grape mass is pretty much complete at that point, and afterward, measurable sugar accretion is said to be 'virtual'—meaning that it is the result of dehydration, causing *agita* among contract growers who sell grapes by weight.

That said, in Michigan's northernmost wine country overall, the decision to balance hang time with climate concerns is similar to a marathon runner who trains all summer and wants to get the race under her belt before flu season hits. Achieving °Bx above 25 is a rare occurrence even in top vintages and the degradation of natural acids is as much a plus in Leelanau and Old Mission viticulture as it is a negative in hotter climates; high TA has been an albatross around the neck of vinifera growers virtually from the outset.

So, the balance that Edson seeks to strike is flavor-ripeness, often seen in the browning of grape seeds as well as tasted in volatile aromatic compounds that appear during the final stages of *véraison*.

According to Dr. Edson, vintage 2014 has struggled with its chemistry final: "It's been a mixed-bag harvest, with the hybrids showing great flavors, but for the *vinifera*, we will have to make necessary adjustments. Chardonnay is low in sugar, high in acid; Pinot Noir will not be suitable for the ripe, rich style I prefer, so it will be used to make a Brut Rosé; sparkling wine can tolerate the lower pH."

For the record, an ideal pH for wine is in the range of 3.5, which (on the logarithmic scale used to measure a solution's ability to donate or accept hydrogen ions) is midway between battery acid and water.

So, for a tasting flight, it may be better to concentrate not on the here and now, and instead, on the there and then:

Starting with a flight of Pinot Grigio—a name that Edson sticks with despite the wine's stylistic resemblance to an Alsatian Pinot Gris more than the crisp, almost herbal wines of Northeast Italy.

It's a marketing game that wine buyers might play, but wine folks won't fall for: Bel Lago Pinot Grigio 2012 is Gris all the way, creamily luscious and soft in the mouth with aromas of peach and yellow plum leading to an earthy minerality. The 'Reserve' from the same vintage mingles honey and spice with the ripe stone fruit; a year in neutral oak barrels adds a touch of smoke and enhances an attractive viscosity of the texture. 2013 is a leaner wine, with a floral and citrus bouquet and light flavors of white Bellini peaches and crushed almonds.

I believe that 2012 was the watershed year for Gewürztraminer in Leelanau; it was the first harvest in which a handful of wine growers up here were able to harmonize its contrarian personalities. Based on a number of factors, a Gewürz may lean toward the flagrantly floral or the markedly musky, and it takes a studied and patient winemaker to help the stars align—one who understands the grape, knows the vineyard's microclimate and soil composition, is willing to allow the hang time required to develop distinctive varietal character and perhaps most importantly, plants the correct clone for the site. Edson's 2012 Gewürz shows all the above; it is a heady nectar resplendent with tropical flavors of mango, grapefruit and a bit of lychee with gardenia and honeysuckle on the nose. But above all, it retains an alacrity and elegance that is nearly impossible to achieve when this grape is grown in warmer climates.

Pinot Noir suffers the same fickle finger of fate, and for the same reasons, which is why California produces very few world-class Pinots and Louisiana, none. Northern Michigan, at the far end of the climate rainbow, requires a conspicuously cooperative year to end up anywhere near the ability to produce a fleshy Pinot with bragging rights. 2014 may not have been the game-winner, but 2010 sure was. Doctor Charlie has 32 unique pinot clones under tillage, and I'm not sure what went into Bel Lago Pinot Noir Reserve 2010, but it worked, resulting in one of the finest Michigan incarnations of this notoriously high-maintenance, prima donna grape—the Maria Callas of viticulture—I've tried. Tightly woven at first whiff, the wine opens within a few minutes of air time, displaying soft, smoky black cherry notes, racy cinnamon and a solid core of classic Burgundian forest-floor.

And then there's Auxerrois, a varietal favored by Charlie's wine-team member Cristin Hosmer and one that has helped to put the grape on America's homegrown wine map. He planted it in 1987 and secured a TTB approval in 1998, six years before Adelsheim—Oregon's Auxerrois ambassador and the only other US winery (that I'm aware of) to produce a 100%, stand-alone varietal wine from the grape.

"My original plan was to use it to shore up Chardonnay in years when I could get the maturity out of those grapes, but I've never had to do that," Edson maintains. "At three-and-a-half tons per acre, it makes a lovely wine on its own."

No argument here: Bel Lago Auxerrois 2012 is endowed with energy, showing ripe pineapple and jasmine on the nose and a richly-ingrained creaminess across the palate, due in part to the year it spent sur lie and the neutral oak in which it was aged. Threads of vanilla and fresh fennel run through the body and linger on the finish, the sort of syncopated structure that vaults this wine into the ranks of can't-miss Leelanau whites.

In fact, tasting through the Bel Lago catalogue, there is a persistent theme running through Doc Aux's wines: Texture. Even those from lesser vintages, which necessarily run thin and sharp, have an underlying framework; an essential and signature fabric. He'll credit hang time; I'll credit a wine scholar who thinks about a glass of wine wearing a horticulturist's trifocals, seeing all aspects of its history, from seed to stemware.

In all, for a wine country which seems often attracted to a homogeneous winemaking style, these selections are exactly what the doctor ordered.

Amy Iezzoni:
National Cherry Queen, Entire 21st Century

Each year in June, the Board of Governors of the National Cherry Festival in Traverse City picks a National Cherry Queen based on intelligence, poise and speaking ability.

And each year since the '80s, they get it wrong.

That's because Traverse City has one (and only one) Cherry Queen, now and *in perpetuum rei memoriam*—Amy Iezzoni, professor of plant breeding at MSU's Department of Horticulture.

Even so, folks discussing the origins of Northern Michigan wine country—people who routinely drop names like Bernie Rink and Ed O'Keefe—have never heard of her. Smug vignoscenti who turn up their noses at cherry wine until they turn down their noses down into a snifter of Leelanau cherry wine, then rave about it, can thank but one person (even before the winemaker): Dr. Amy, whose introduction of the sweet-tart Balaton cherry to commercial fruit production has raised the cherry wine bar so high that I defy the most snobbish among you to dismiss it as 'one dimensional'.

"Prior to the development of Balaton, the sour cherry industry in the US was a monoculture of a French variety called Montmorency," says Amy. "One of our missions has been to make that industry more diverse, specifically by breeding cultivars with better fruit quality, better disease resistance and more consistent yields. Currently, we run an aggressive breeding program with about 25 acres of seedlings and 15 test sites around the country. Balaton was our first introduction."

Balaton began as an unpronounceable variety that Amy discovered on a trip to Hungary, where the cherry culture is so rabid that the average hungry Hungarian consumes eleven times more fruit than an American. Originally, she says, the variety of Hungarian landrace cherries was astonishing, but when the Communists took the reins after World War II and the agricultural industry became collectivized, commercial objectives soon outweighed diversity. The tree that was ultimately cherry-picked from the lot was called Ujfehértói Fürtös. Compared to

Montmorency, this particular mouthful is sweeter, firmer, redder, and as an undeniable bonus, makes an intriguingly complex table wine—due in part to its ability to reach a °Bx 24, roughly on par with local *vinifera* grapes.

In fact, the only drawback to the drinkable drupe was its jaw-breaking name.

"We knew that Ujfehértói Fürtös wouldn't cut it, so—with the approval of the Hungarians—we named it after Lake Balaton, the largest freshwater lake in Hungary."

Which, happily, happens to be the only word in the entire Uralic language family that Americans can pronounce.

As you can imagine, there is only one thing that could make Amy Iezzoni's decades-long love affair with *Prunus cerasus* complete: A *ménage à trois* with a winemaker.

And along came Charlie 'I Like Sunsets, Long Walks on the Beach, Puppy Breath and Talking About S-RNase-Based Gametophytic Self-Incompatibility' Edson, the whiz-kid behind Bel Lago winery and the creator of the best cherry wine on the Leelanau Peninsula. By default, you know what that means, right? Since Leelanau grows the best wine cherries in the world, and thus, produces the best cherry wine in the world, it means that in an unassuming tasting room a few miles outside of unassuming Cedar, Michigan, on the western shore of podunk Lake Leelanau, for around fifteen bucks, you can purchase a global superlative.

But first, in order to truly enjoy it, you have to face down the Nelly Negatives: Cherry wine is the Dangerfield of drinks. Mention it to sommeliers and you don't need to consult Rasmussen to know that the majority of them will tell you that cherry wine is something that Tommy James and The Shondels swig with total strangers or that Jermaine Stewart guzzles as a substitute for sloppy sex while George Thorogood howls about it in the same breath as hot peppers and *ooh-hoo-hooeee.*

To their point, of course, when Van Morrison gets loaded along the Cyprus Avenue train tracks, it ain't on '89 Beaucastel.

But those are the dregs of the drupe drink—decent cherry wine is hardly a low-rent bevvie, and the descriptor most often used is 'cherry pie in a glass' for the unusual array of spices that are often a natural component of the wine's profile. Edson treats his cherry wine with the same care and think-too-much compulsion as he does with grape wine, but the beautiful thing is that cherries ripen a good three months before the hundred or so grape varieties he grows.

This is just a theory, mind you, but do you know how the first born in a given family tends to have certain advantages in life, due in part to the coddling attention of his or her proud parents? Maybe the same holds true for the first vinified juice of Charlie's wine season.

For whatever reason, Bel Lago Cherry Wine is a sensory smorgasbord: Vivid ruby in the glass with a perfumed bouquet—cherry jam with clove and cedar scents—while on the palate, it is velvety and pure, showing plum preserves and fruit compote cut with toasted hazelnut, soft tannins and a bracing undertow of acidity.

GOOD HARBOR®
Cherry Wine
Michigan

A Semi Sweet Wine, Alcohol 10% By Volume, Produced and Bottled By
Good Harbor Vineyards, Lake Leelanau, Michigan 49653 BW-MI-49

That would be the art end of cherry wine. For the equation's business end, the man to see is Sam Simpson, whose family has been growing tart cherries in Leelanau since the 1970s. In the day, Sam's grandfather John Worth Simpson (1917–2002) had a four hundred acre cherry orchard outside Leland; the industry was flush and prices were high.

Today, the Simpson's cherry acreage has dwindled to 120; the industry is flushable and prices are about the same as they were in the '70s.

"We're getting out of commodity farming," he says firmly, but somewhat wistfully, "and a lot of it comes down to the decisions on the CIAB. The board has too much power and the tart cherry industry up here has suffered accordingly."

Simpson means the Cherry Industry Administrative Board; *'an appallingly stupid creation of the USDA'* according to Food Law & Policy professor Baylen Linnekin of George Mason University Law School. The CIAB web site maintains that the board exists to 'match the current year's supply with the historical demand for tart cherry products, helping to insure an appropriate volume of cherries moves to the market in those years of overproduction'.

Leaving such decisions up to bureaucrats instead of farmers doesn't even sound good on paper, and in the field, in bumper-crop years, it often equates to tons of salable cherries being dumped on the ground. Prices per pound, says Sam, may range from 45¢ to a low of 15¢, at which point it becomes cheaper to compost the fruit than to process it.

Adding insult to that injury, the final price is not determined until after the cherries are sold, and Simpson—whose last year as a commodity farmer was 2009, didn't receive a check for that crop until 2011.

According to the USDA, the regulated industry consists of about 600 tart cherry growers and 40 tart cherry handlers. Meanwhile, about three-quarters of America's tart cherry output comes from Michigan, so any negative impact from federal regulations hits us here first and hardest.

Thank God for wine, huh?

"We lease our acres now, but reserve three blocks of cherry trees specifically for wine," says Sam. "That's around twenty acres. Ounce for ounce these days, wine makes more economic sense up here in Leelanau, especially since grapes have raised land prices; wine grapes are the high utility produce, so the market drives this land into wine fruit. Wine is the way to go. "

That is, if you have the know how—and Sam Simpson does. His grandfather established Good Harbor Winery outside Leland in 1980, which his father Bruce enriched, enlivened and expanded until his untimely passing in 2009. Sam and his sister Taylor, under the guidance of their mother Debbie, have kept the winery in the forefront of the wine industry in Leelanau. In fact, Good Harbor's cherry wine was the first inkling I had that the plebian plonk of my childhood—Boone's Farm Wild Cherry—might have picked itself up by the bootstraps and come of age.

"We'll do around fourteen thousand gallons in 2014," Sam declares, while behind him, Taylor checks his figures against a computer print-out. "That's around 100 tons of fruit; 3800 cases."

He tells me that cherry wine is evolving, improving, and the experimenting never ends. Currently, he's using five different fruit yeasts in different lots and will decide the final blend at bottling time.

If he has any 'secret' to the singular scrumptiousness of his cherry wine, he claims it is the Balaton cherry—80% of his wine's fruit content.

So, in the end, it's all back to Dr. Queen Amy Iezzoni and her hedonistic, Hungarian horticultural hubris.

The future? Cherry breeding is a time-consuming endeavor and note-taking from seedling through a tree's life-cycle takes decades. And once the specific cultivars that show the most promise are determined, you still have to convince farmers to plant them. That said, Dr. Amy is singing the praises of two new varieties called Danube and Jubilee.

Although they are not grown on any large scale, she suggests that a bushel or three may wind up in Charlie Edson's cherry wine.

That would explain (to me anyway) why his wines reach such a remarkable depth of complexity, why he holds a royal flush in the poker game of enology and why life with the Edson/Iezzonis is a bottomless bowl of cherries.

The Intoxicating Intellect Of
G. Stanley Howell

Had G. Stanley Howell showed up for our wine chat dressed in full CSA officer regalia, complete with three star collar insignia, cadet grey overcoat and lion's-head saber, I would have considered it perfectly appropriate. Not only because the retired Professor and Viticulturist Emeritus at Michigan State University is a dead-ringer for Robert E. Lee (he is) but because he embodies all the qualities of gentleness, elegance, humility and insane intelligence that I imagine were manifest in the original Marble Man.

Take, for example, the above-referenced three-star collar (denoting the rank of Confederate Colonel) that Lee wore throughout his Generalship; an iconic show of modesty. Likewise, Dr. Howell scoffs at the praise I heap liberally upon his name, suggesting that the genuine credit for having jump-started Michigan's wine industry may belong to Nate Stackhouse of Warner Vineyards who, along with his degree from UC Davis, laid the foundation of Howell's wine-savviness:

"Before I met Nate, I didn't know jack about winemaking; I was a Southern boy, weaned directly from mother's milk to sour mash whiskey."

And like any good research biologist, he is willing to own up to mistakes he's made through life's middle-ground of wine, summing up his career like this: "A lot of what I did was self-preservation. For the most part, I couldn't afford many errors. If I get 999 things correct, nobody remembers. If I get a single thing wrong, nobody forgets."

Well, Vicksburgs or vineyards, Ol' Dixie or °Brixie, the most important difference between Lee and Howell is that when it came to their own personal life-defining, legacy-securing campaign, Robert E. Lee lost.

And G. Stanley Howell won.

§

Howell's father was a carpenter with an eighth-grade education, and the intense and respectful way that Stan describes the old man's skill betrays his lifelong wonder at the mechanisms behind art, whether it's a cabinet or a cabernet, an end table or a table wine. Howell grew up in the deepest part of the Deep South near Mobile, Alabama, graduating from high school in the late 1950s and doing his undergraduate work at Mississippi State University, Starkville. After obtaining his Ph.D. in Horticulture from the University of Minnesota, he joined the faculty at Michigan State University in 1969 and set out to research, among other things, the physiological and cultural factors limiting vine growth. But it wasn't wine grape vines he was focusing upon back then: He recalls his early work with Welch's, which has its second largest grape juice plant in Lawton, Michigan. At the time, he was trying to find methods of reducing labor in the field.

Not that there were many wine grape vineyards to worry about, of course. In 1969, Michigan's wine industry was a bit of an embarrassment, and if you were to say it was in its 'infancy', you'd have to reference Rosemary's Baby—that's how diabolically awful most of these wines were. 95% of them were classified as 'dessert' wines, meaning that they were molar-crumblers made from Concord or Niagara grapes, heavily sweetened and selling for under a dollar a bottle.

This was a time when a 'sophisticated' wine for most Detroiters was 'Cold Duck'—an invention of Harold Borgman of the upscale Ponchartrain Hotel, which followed an old German tradition of blending champagne and leftover wine. Apparently, 'cold ends' in German is *kalte ende*, which is a single consonant away from *kalte ente*, meaning 'Cold Duck'.

If that story is apocryphal or true I know not, but I recall my mother describing it as tasting like a blend of Faygo Red Pop, Ocean Spray CranGrape and André Champagne.

Not in dispute is that the sparkling wine used in the Cold Duck that the Ponchartrain served (exclusively for 50 years according to Borgman's grandson) was made by Bronte Champagne Company, one of the first Michigan wineries to open after Prohibition. And it was Bronte's winemaker, Angelo Spinazze, who Howell credits for having seeded the idea of an MSU program to evaluate various cold-hardy cultivars that could be used to produce a higher end Michigan wine.

"When I first floated the idea at the school, however, I encountered plenty of administrative roadblocks—any research that promoted the alcohol industry was off limits. In fact, I was told quietly that pursuing such a program was career suicide. Fortunately, later that same year we had a changing of the guard in the Dean's office, and Dr. Larry Boger came on board as a very broad thinker. He was receptive, and paved the way for our first experiments vineyard where we established a number of cold-resistant cultivars that had seen success in the Finger Lakes region of New York."

The conundrum that Howell then faced was cultural more than viticultural; 'prevailing wisdom' can be as limiting a factor in agronomy as climate. Local folklore suggested that 'good' wine was simply wine whose raw material grew easily, and so the hurdle of convincing growers to extend beyond the Big Three—Concord, Niagara and Delaware grapes (all *Vitis labrusca*)—was a major one.

The answer was hybrids—grapes engineered genetically for taste, yield and hardiness, and generally created by crossing frost/disease resistent native American species *Vitis riparia* or *Vitis labrusca* with tender, but more flavorful European *Vitis vinifera*. While new red-wine species like Baco Noir and Maréchal Foch could withstand nearly everything that a Michigan January could throw at them, weaning growers from the tried-and-true was an obstacle nearly impossible to overcome.

Until the establishment of Spartan Cellars, that is—an experimental MSU campus winery which involved itself in all aspects of winemaking, from planting and vineyard management to laboratory analyses. Although these wines were never intended for commercial consumption, they were treated as if they were, allowing Michigan growers a real-time experience of what was possible.

"The establishment of Spartan Cellars was crucial," Howell insists. "It had been an idea long in germination before it finally came to fruition in 1973. It was a required move for the sort of research results we were having. Hard to say if it would work today—then, the Michigan wine industry was small and we were able to hold professional tastings for Michigan wineries, and nearly all would come. I liked it because planting, vinifying and selling our experiments was their area of expertise. This took me out of the loop; they chose what they wanted to grow."

Among the varieties that showed the most appeal to local farmers were Vignoles and Vidal Blanc, white wine hybrids that provide a remarkable array of sophisticated flavors and are open to many stylistic interpretations. Among Howell's favorites which fared less well was Chardonel, a hybrid's hybrid with a parentage of Seyval and Chardonnay.

"Chardonel never took off, which I thought was a shame," says Howell. "It epitomized the sort of cultivar we were trying to popularize, with superior sugars, the right amount of acidity, high productivity and cold hardiness. Plus, it can be vinified in a multitude of styles—stainless-steel fermentation makes a crisp wine, but it responds equally well to oak and has wonderful green apple notes that make it ideal for sparkling wine. And I recall, when it was under testing in the vineyard, we had a huge hail storm two weeks before harvest and the Chardonel vines did quite well."

The market nibbled, but it didn't bite, and in 2014, I can only find a single Michigan winery—Tabor Hill—which produces a stand-alone Chardonel.

That what *should* sell doesn't always sell was one of several epiphanies that Stan Howell had as he learned on the job. For example, his initial conviction was that for any European varietal to succeed commercially anywhere, it required a 170 day growing season. And not only that, but needed certain climactic parameters that he was certain ruled out varieties that are now doing pretty well here, including late-ripeners like Cabernet Franc—even, he confesses, cold-weather grapes like Riesling. When, nursing his personal passion for German whites he accompanied Ed O'Keefe (Chateau Grand Traverse) to a trip to Germany in 1973, he returned to plant Riesling in Lansing, where it promptly succumbed to winter kill—reaffirming his theory.

Of course he admits now that he'd left two variables from his formula: Old Mission Peninsula and Ed O'Keefe—a man to whom Michigan, quite arguably, owes its modern *vinifera* culture.

"Ed found—or created—microclimates two hundred miles north of Lansing where Riesling could not only survive, but flourish. He is, for good reason, a driving force in Michigan wine: A strong personality combined with classic entrepreneurial drive. We are blessed to have him here and could probably use a few more from the same mold."

Indeed, Chateau Grand Traverse's consistently award-winning Rieslings, which continues to wow vignoscenti worldwide, would ultimately form the foundation of a single milepost which has defined Michigan viticulture ever since:

"Since it's now been proven that we *can* grow *vinifera* here, we *have* to grow *vinifera* here," Stan Howell maintains, "even if the right locations are somewhat nip and tuck. A winery with ambition must make two kinds of wine—wine that makes their reputation and wine that pays the bills. If your name is Rothschild, it can be the same wine, but if you are anybody else, you'll probably have to make different wines for each category."

The brass ring for the state's reputation-making, he believes, is in proprietary blends—much (ironically) as it has been for the Rothschilds. Even his prized Chardonel, virtually unexplored as a stand-alone, is a silent partner in a lot of Michigan white wines:

"One of the realities of Michigan's wine is the hard sell of varietal hybrids. I have come to understand a few realities: First, most wines in a given style are improved by blending and second, it is smarter and better to create a proprietary blended wine than to try to educate a doubtful public regarding a 'new' and previously unknown variety. While I believe this is true for nearly all wines, including *vinifera*, it is especially true of hybrids and allows a potential customer to evaluate the qualities of the wine in the glass and its cost/unit to determine its value. I suspect that here, quite a lot of Chardonel goes into such blends."

And so, the refined and gentile Southern gentleman (who has moved through the opposing Northern forces of climate and disease and deployed wine varieties that have altered the field of battle irrevocably and ultimately prevailing in the War Between The Grapes), remains ever gracious in victory. If there's an Appomattox, it may well be his old research laboratory at MSU, where the terms of the truce between weather and wine are largely his own doing. Proof may be best seen in the statistics given earlier: Whereas in 1969, 95% of Michigan wines were essentially super-sweet dessert styles, in 2014, 95% are not.

Yet, G. Stanly Howell insists that he'd never have made it as a commercial winemaker:

"A successful grape grower secures the best current knowledge regarding location, site, variety, training and trellis choice, canopy management and crop control, and ruthlessly applies such practices. I would be terrible as a farmer, not for lack of knowing the right things to do, but from my interminable 'tinkering' and asking 'what if?'"

"No, I have been better for Michigan as a *vine dreamer*."

TONY CICCONE:
PAPA CAN TOO PREACH

I wonder if when Tony's kids were small, they used to say, *"Papa, tell us the dead cat story again!!"*

Actually, you probably know at least one of Tony's kids—pretty well, too—but enough about that for now. I'm of an age to be one of Tony's kids, and every time I interview him, like a tot on his old man's knee, I pester him to tell me the dead cat story again.

And every time he tells it, I laugh my *culo* off.

See, when Tony was growing up in an Italian enclave in Aliquippa in western Pennsylvania, the six Ciccone boys (known locally as 'The Zero Brothers' because their names all ended in an 'o') had no sisters and as a result, had to learn all the household chores—ironing, bread making, sewing and so on. One of young Tony's jobs was to monitor the wine barrels bubbling away in the cellar, which was a vital gig in any self-respecting do-it-yourself Italian household. One day, he's checking the wine and he finds that a neighborhood cat has fallen into a barrel and drowned and he immediately runs to tell his father. "So take it out already," Silvio—fifty years a mill worker at Jones & Laughlan Steel—insisted.

And Tony claims that they drank it anyway, with no one the wiser.

At 84, Tony (Silvio Jr.) Ciccone has strained and drained many a wine barrel since, and it is fair to say that in the intervening years, his quality restrictions have grown while the pet-allowance factor has shrunk. He's now the helmsman of Ciccone Vineyard, an estate-focused winery overlooking West Grand Traverse Bay in the Leelanau Peninsula, producer of (among a host of *vinifera* and hybrids) Michigan's only Dolcetto. Like the cat from the vat, you can take the Italian out of the enclave, but you can't...

The path that took Tony from his tight Pennsylvania hood to the wilds of Leelanau, felines to grapevines, was a convoluted one. After high school he joined the Air Force and was stationed in the Aleutian

Islands—about as far away from the grit and grime and bowling alleys of Western Pennsylvania steel country as he could manage. In fact, in outlook more than distance, so was Geneva College, rated among the top ten regional colleges in the country by *US News & World Report*: His degree in physics—for which he is still called 'The Professor'—was a direction not many sons of mill workers took. After that, however, Tony went the way of any good Italian kid in the Fifties: He married a Catholic girl named Madonna Louise and began making babies. Eight in total, of which two—Paula and Mario—are now employed at the vineyard; Paula learning the winemaking ropes and Mario managing the vineyards. These two, though ever-present and starring in Ciccone Winery: The Next Generation, may not be the Ciccone you know.

Tony put in his braniac years developing tanks for Chrysler's defense division, indispensable for the high-priority M1 Abrams tank which remains, to this day, the principal battle tank of the United States Army. When Iacocca sold the division, Tony transferred to General Dynamics as an electro-optical engineer and began working on guided missiles and other rocket-sciencey projects. Tragically, in the interim, his wife died and left him with a handful of—well, handfuls; a bevy of bambinos with wills as strong as his own. Ultimately, he married Joan, who remains by his side to this day, forty-eight years later; a foundational figure in the winery.

Joan has been an anchor of whom he cannot speak highly enough. The going, at times, has been rough. "This is a passion that requires a well-rounded sort of dedication," he points out, "because the business parameters of winemaking are quite different than the vineyard parameters. That means competing with the world while maintaining a focus on Michigan wine, and that includes dealing with seasonal disasters like last winter; unfortunately, the bills don't stop coming in just because the grapes don't grow."

The example he gives is as irrefutable as a physics equation: Powdery mildew, a yearly scourge to these valiant vintners on the 45th parallel, needs yearly treatment whether the vine's fruit sets or not; the same labor and materials are required if it's boom or bust.

"And 2014 is pretty much a bust," Tony admits. "We still have to spend the thousands of dollars to spray, and without fruit, you might as well be spraying the shoulder of the road. But it has to be done. I think you'll see a lot more wineries for sale up here after the stock from '12/'13 is gone; there are just so many slices of the pie the region can handle, and in poor vintages, everybody scrambles for juice, driving prices up. Not everyone can—or cares to—swing it."

One constant I have noticed about Ciccone wines each time I visit is that, with allowances for vintage variation, they keep getting better and better. When I first tried Tony's Dolcetto, the vines were infants and the wine showed as simple and acidic; now, it is sleek and refined with a sensational bouquet of cherries and lightly toasted almonds. Some of this is vine age, of course—older plants with deeper roots tend to make wines that are more complex—but the rest of it is Tony's re-earning his physicist's degree over and over again. He is a compulsive tinkerer and is never entirely satisfied. Now, every winemaker makes the same claim, I know, but I have watched the direction of this winery's wares and it has been rationally consistent—not unlike the M1 tank, as it happens, which began development in the mid-Sixties and did not enter U.S. service until 1980. Slow and steady wins the race, whether its warfare or winefare.

Not that there is any flash or exuberance missing; these wines are easy to enjoy, bright with pure fruit and multi-layered with Michigan terroir. But, with Tony, there is also a growing sense of nostalgia in these wines; his labels and wine names often pay homage to loved ones, living and dead—his mother, his wife, his daughters.

Guido, Rocco, Niello, Guitano and Pietro have gone before and he is the last remaining Zero Brother, but he speaks with obvious pride about his grandson, another Silvio. Of Paula's winemaking, he says: "When you get to arguing about process, you know you've taught her it right."

And incidentally, unless you have recently returned from an interstellar vacation, Tony's eldest daughter (named after her mother Madonna) is probably the kid you know.

As for Tony—the papa who wasn't supposed to preach—if he's getting tired of telling *The Cat In The Vat*, he doesn't let that particular cat out of the bag. He looks fondly out of his window, surveying his fourteen acres, and when I ask him if he still makes wine in the cellar he spreads his arms at the the sprawling vineyards and the big red barn beyond and answers, "Sure. Only now, that's my cellar."

Preach it, Papa.

WHERE SWISS CHEESE IS HOLY: RACLETTE-MAKING IN SUTTON'S BAY

The only thing more mid-America wholesome than church-going is cheese-making, so it's fitting that John and Anne Hoyt—after years of bouncing around temporary Leelanau digs—landed inside the defunct Sutton's Baby Bible Church. Although it must be said, I can understand how you could go belly-up producing labor-intensive artisan cheese in a style most Michiganders have never heard of, but how do you flop as a church?

No matter; so far, the score is God - 0, Raclette - 1.

The story begins in the pastoral hills of Valais, Switzerland, home to half of Swiss wine production as well as ground zero for Raclette—the semi-soft cheese whose eponymous dish is a culinary mainstay of this small, landlocked country. Both Valaisian traditions combined to make John and Anne Hoyt; he was an exchange student from Detroit learning French while picking up seasonal work in the vineyards; she was a cowgirl from France doing seasonal work in the alpages of the Swiss mountains. They met in 1986 at one of the many Swiss junctions where these two culture cultures meet and, finding that he had had more interest in caseiculture than viticulture, John went to Chateauneuf School in Valais to earn his cheese degrees.

After stints at several respected Swiss dairy co-ops, John and Anne traveled to Oregon, where John's brother had a contact at Springfield Creamery (owned by author Ken Kesey's family) and from there, to Omena, Michigan in the Leelanau Peninsula where John used his European-honed pruning skills at Boskydel, L. Mawby, Leelanau Cellars and Good Harbor, socking away nickels and dimes and on the lookout for a stainless steel pasteurizing vat so that the couple could pursue their one and true love.

"I finally found one in a neighbor's basement; original purpose unknown," John says, "but it was a steel-jacketed vat the right size to pasteurize enough milk to make eight wheels of raclette per day—our goal at the time. We set up shop in an unused room next to Keith Brown's Omena Harbor bar. It used to be a gas station bay, so we had to clean the oil off the floors and fire up the boiler in the basement for heat. That went well enough; I paid Keith a couple hundred dollars a month for use of the stalls and a percentage of sales."

A workable business plan until Brown sold the bar and the new owner neglected to pay the utility bills. Cheesemaking, besides being a sterile proposition, requires precise temperature control. "We were reduced to bringing in propane tanks to run the operation, and that got old pretty quickly."

Add to that the stress of hauling milk up from Garvin Farms in Cedar in the back of his Ranger, nine cans at a time, and the future of Leelanau Cheese hung in the balance.

It was finally tipped by Lee Lutes, who in 2000 was (and is) the winemaker at Black Star Farms. The cheeseworks relocated to the Farm, where Anne and John acidified, coagulated and separated curds from whey in full view of a semi-tipsy crowd in the winery tasting room. They tripled production, upping the ante to 24 wheels per vat every couple days and found retail outlets that essentially bought every pound they didn't sell through Black Star's lively souvenir shop.

That lasted for fourteen years—and I recall it being a mandatory stop in Sutton's Bay for plenty of those years. Whatever happened I am not a party to—somebody cheesed somebody off, who knows?—maybe it was just time to move on—but the new operation is in the repurposed sacellum, where the sprawling ex-prayer room serves the mission perfectly.

Had John Cleese wandered into Leelanau Cheese, his conversation with John and Anne Hoyt might have progressed exactly as it did in the classic Monty Python sketch; there's no Caerphilly, Perle de Champagne, Gorgonzola, Camembert or Mozzarella—certainly no Venezuelan Beaver Cheese—and of the thirty-seven other cheeses the customer requests in his frustrating television attempt to cheese-up, he makes no mention of Raclette. Too bad: If he had, he'd have walked out a happy man. Like Germany and wine, Leelanau Cheese makes only one product and makes it better than anyone else.

Don't take my word for it, though. The American Cheese Society awarded John and Anne *Best of Show* in 2007 and at the Michigan State Fair, they're seven times champions. Follow-up awards from the Wisconsin-sponsored U.S. Championship Cheese Contest must have been like a California wine winning the Judgment of Paris in 1976.

So, what is Raclette? Like most people, I thought it was the name of the 1970s melted-cheese party dish like fondue rather than the cheese itself, but it turns out that 'Raclette' day was a lazy one for whoever names meals. Raclette is classified as either semi-soft or semi-hard (as riesling—an ideal accompaniment—can be labeled 'semi-dry' or 'semi-sweet' depending on the marketing strategy) and is characterized by an edible, nut-brown crust that forms after a brine bath and an inoculation of yeast and coryneform bacteria; the cheese then undergoes a period of cellar aging during which it is washed with salt water daily.

In the ideal wheel, the interior is smooth, ivory-colored and gently piquant with flavors of buttery hazelnuts, herbs and resplendent with earthy complexity. Melted, preferably before a roaring hearth fire and requisite in serving Raclette-the-meal, it becomes velvety and runny and traditionally accompanies small Valaisian potatoes and gherkins.

Unwilling to be labeled one-trick-ponies, the Hoyts produce not one, but two presentations of Raclette, neither made from pony milk. The 'sharp' version undergoes prolonged aging in order to ripen; up to ten months in a temperature and humidity controlled environment.

On the day I visited, work was underway to construct a massive steel-and-concrete cellar in the rear of the property, which, when completed, will be to cheesemaking what the Large Hadron Collider is to particle physics—both inventions of the Swiss, by the way. Age-time is always a delicate balance between spoilage and improveage; that's why it has to be approached with such surgical precision. Done correctly, a transformation of casein proteins and milk fat into a complex mix of amino acids, amines and fatty acids happens gradually, turning a mild, milky young cheese into a graceful oldster filled with character and depth. The tang of aldehydes and alpha-keto acids offer a sensory experience that is often called 'sharp', although like 'Reserve' on a wine label, there is no industry standard for such a designation. In any case,

Leelanau Cellars' aged Raclette offers an array of variations on a theme: Beneath the taffy-colored rind, the pungency is more pronounced, the nuttiness nuttier and the richness redoubled in a slightly drier package; there is a savory weight to it that seems almost meat-like. For the extra two and a half bucks a pound, it is well worth it.

When asked why he has not branched out into other cheese varieties—through curiosity, if nothing else—John Hoyt gave me the same sort of puzzled stare that Michael Palin did when asked if he carried Cheddar, the most popular cheese in the world; a look that said, "Not much call for it around these parts." In fact, cheddaring—an add-on process in cheesemaking wherein the curds are kneaded and stacked—is something requiring extra time, extra space and extra practice, none of which the Hoyts are currently able to invest.

"I would like to try my hand at Gruyère," he admits, naming the other, similar quintessentially Swiss cheese, which is a little like a Pinot Blanc maker saying he'd like to branch out into Pinot Gris.

For now, we'll have to settle for the Raclette and the Cheesus puns; the glittery highbrow and the guttery lowbrow that makes Leelanau Cheese Co. such a Pythonesque paradigm.

Adam Satchwell:
Cracking The Lychee Nut

Some people fall in love with shy, retiring types—Marian the Librarian or Johnny Accountant. Some folks prefer introverted intellectuals; others go for partners with personalities that dominate whatever room they're in.

Ditto goes for wine. For some, the ideal bottle is filled with understated and gentle juice; a modest tipple with a light bouquet—an unassuming presence at the soirée. Others want a wine with some meat on her bones. They're after an oily, perfumed ball-buster with an overbearing attitude; a soul sweet enough to crumble molars but muscular enough to pulverize spines. That's when the old Fräulein, The She-Wolf of

Strasbourg, her Grand Ducal Highness Lady Gewürztraminer gets the booty call.

Alas, for wine growers, even she does not always put out on the first date.

How about the fifth date, Adam Satchwell? Because nobody in Michigan knows the answer better than you.

Adam is the dude who puts the shady in Shady Lanes; one of Leelanau's old guard wine folks and top producers of cool-climate *vininfera.* He came to chilly Grand Traverse wine country in 2000 and has played an integral role in developing the area's reputation from a frosty, quirky peninsula to world-class wine country.

As the recent 'City of Riesling' weekend proved, Northern Michigan has earned a spotlight on the world's stage as a producer of elegant, nuanced and age-worthy Rieslings that can make waves among the oceans of wine produced at the grape's main stomping ground, Germany.

It would stand to reason (at least in my mind) that we should be able to create equally compelling wine from the mutated Alsatian Traminer love child.

And yet, for the very reasons I overblew in the opening, Gewürz is not everybody's cup of porch pounder. At its voluptuous prime, it makes a wine that is filled with aromas and flavors unlike any other; it shows big notes of sweet tangerine, oily, intense floral bouquets (which is why they are called 'bouquets')—roses, primarily—grapefruit, and above all, lychee nut, with which it shares a very distinct monoterpene called cis-rose oxide.

Which, to digress, is an interesting chemistry lesson for wine tasters: Nearly all the scents you pull from a snifter and identify as pineapple or apple or peach—or lychee or rose—are, in fact, the very same chemicals that make those fruits smell and taste like they do. Mother Nature doles out her cornucopia with a certain, delightful frugality.

In any case, Gewürztraminer is to wine what Jennifer Lopez's badonkadonk is to pulchritutidy; brobdingnagian, bountiful, beautiful—but not to every waif-cravin' heroin-chic-lovin' drinker's taste. Plus, it is hard to pronounce. As a result, there's no ready market for it, and it has been an ongoing pet experiment among a few Northern Michigan winemakers, but one which had not, in my various samplings, yet climbed out of the test tube and come to life.

And then I tried Shady Lane Gewürztraminer, 2012, and on came the Super Arc klieg lights, center stage. Apparently, based on my snort, the fifth date is the charm: The wine is superb; concentrated and potent, showing sweet mandarin orange, pronounced rose petals, exotic tropical fruits and in the mouth, the pure and clean lycheeness of lychee—nothing else tastes like this. I concluded that for whatever combination of reasons—clones, climate, cleverness and/or a cluster of clues finally clicking—this wine is living proof that the nut's been cracked: Gewürztraminer has found a unique home in the peninsula and may ultimate muscle her way to a leading role.

"It was a long journey and it took several years," Satchwell admits. "There are a lot of inherent pitfalls with this grape. Bitterness, high pH and especially, balance: With the multitude of unique aromatics and flavors inside Gewürztraminer, there's a danger of over expression of one component at the expense of another."

Luck and wisdom served him from the outset, however, when he chose to plant the two (then) available clones of the cultivar—called, like those goofy little *Cat In The Hat* sidekicks, 'One' and 'Two'. "I planted in 2004, and the first harvest, in 2007, I vinified bone dry. I liked it, and so did about two other people. It was parental pride mostly—the wine was prey to all the dangers I was worried about; the phenolics were out of whack. It showed promise, but needed work."

2008 was not the year either; the fruit didn't set, the crop was dismal and he wound up purchasing grapes from a neighboring vineyard. In 2009 nature was a tad more cooperative and he finished the wine at about 1% residual sugar, allowing some of the subtle, sweet citrus and gingerbread flavors—showing vine maturity—to surface.

2010 and 2011's wine came across as excessively floral however, with the rose-oil terpenes running a bit amuck (as you might expect of One and Two). He spoke to growers in Alsace, re-thought his canopy management, and voilà—2012 produced a wine where every contrasting odorizers and flavonoids decided to settle down, take their seats and listen to the professor. They only speak in turns, and then dutifully and only when called upon.

Is Adam Satchwell's 2012 Shady Lane Gewürztraminer the equal of those from the Grand Crus of Domaine René Muré, Willm, Zind-Humbrecht or Pierre Frick? Not hardly. But these great estates have been breaking the sandstone and schist for hundreds of years through many generations. Adam is taking reams of notes along with the rest of the class.

"One thing I noticed in 2012—for the first time since planting—the berries from each of the two clones showed a remarkable difference: In

Clone One, the classic rose notes dominated, while in Clone Two, it was the lychee flavors. This can only be down to vine age. In the early and mid-fermentation process, the must threw off new, odd scents of banana and the waxy wrappers from Bazooka Joe bubblegum, but these turned out to be 'precursor' scents and settled into a nice, rounded spice."

The learning curve is remarkable, and although last winter was the most severe test of the appellation's ability to recover from a really savage season, Satchwell's vineyards—including the frost-susceptible Gewürz—were down, but not for the count. And neither were the winemakers.

Of course, I'd expect no less from Adam Satchwell—a persevering pioneer on this plucky, polar promontory.

TURNING ON THE PICOTT SPICOT
IN THE 'CITY OF RIESLING'

Or: *'Sour Grapes: Memoire of a TC Weekend'*

For a place that bills itself as the City of Riesling, Traverse City spends a lot of time sleeping with the enemy. For example, browse the tree-lined heart of the shopping district and look for chocolate covered grapes at

Riesling Republic; try to find Riesling-flavored balsamic vinegar at Fustini's or Riesling fudge at Murdick's. Guess what? You'll strike out. Go on a quest for Riesling popcorn, dried Riesling, Riesling sorbet, Riesling milkshakes? Zero. Nor is there is a sportswear shop called Riesling Hill Boutique or a Riesling Cone ice cream parlor. In the window of the camera shop, that silly smiley-face icon—which everybody knows is bile-yellow by birth—has not been transformed into a gentle seafoam Riesling green, but into blood-colored—and dare I say Commie-approved—red.

Sorry, whoever thought of the poetic nickname 'City of Riesling' for Traverse City; the merchants, whistle-stopping politicians and founding fathers aren't buying into it. To them, TC will always be Metropolis of Montmorency, Port Prunus Cerasus, Cherryville U.S.A., and as a result, Riesling is the Bonny Prince Charlie of Fruit: An ignominious pretender.

None of which matters to Mr. Riesling himself, although clearly, it should. To Stuart Pigott, revered as the world's foremost expert on Riesling—the grape that puts the fine wine in the Rhine, the pizzazz in the Alsazz and the thumbs up in Finger Lakes—life is just a bowl of Johannisberger Rheinriesling.

§

July 26, 2014: This evening, I fetched Pigott from the TC landing strip—which is not, lest you doubt the sincerity of my opening lament, called Riesling Capital Airport—and deposited him with his sponsor Amanda Danielson of The Franklin. Pigott was in town to host a screening of his film *'WATCH YOUR BACK: The Riesling Movie'* and star in a Horizon Book signing of his new book. *'Best White Wine On Earth'*—which, surprisingly, in his studied opinion, is not made from la *méthode saignée* juice from Traverse City cherries.

Anyway, Pigott is hardly an unknown author—he has written a slew of wine books and is a columnist for the *Frankfurter Allgemeine Zeitung*, which he claims is Germany's equivalent of *The New York Times*. Even so, I fear that your average happy-go-lucky, Traverse-City-vacationing, up-from-Grand-Rapids yuckster likely reads neither one, and I can say from experience that there is no sadder circumstance on earth for a writer than sitting in a bookstore hoping someone wants an autograph.

Strike that: I just thought of a circumstance on earth sadder than that for a writer, but I'll save it for later.

Long before any book signings or movie screenings, I had the opportunity to interview Stuart Pigott and to tap into his vast Riesling knowledge by employing *méthode saignée* to his brain pan. And also to tease him about his sports coat—mostly because, based on his fluency in German I assumed he was German, and when I was looking for him in the airport I singled him out by employing a generally foolproof method of identifying a Berlin journalist amid a maelstrom of Midwesterners: An Aryan fashion statement. Indeed, the loudest, red plaid jacket in the crowd turned out to be worn by Stuart Pigott and I was forthwith shocked to discover that Pigott is, in fact, British.

Even so, that shock was no match for Amanda's expression when I cracked wise-ass about his hemorrhage-colored tartan during the interview—I don't imagine her jaw would have dropped quicker if I had announced that I was actually a drug journalist in town to score some Riesling-flavored heroin.

In any case, the social awkwardness faded like a snort of unleaded premium in a Trockenbeerenauslese, and Stuart Pigott proceeded to school me mightily in why he believes that Riesling is a superior wine grape to say, Scuppernong or Muscadine.

For starters, he insists, unadorned and unbastardized by corporate mad men, Riesling simply produces a better-tasting wine—a wine simultaneously refreshing in its simplicity and (when done correctly) nearly unplumbable in its profundity. Having already telegraphed disdain for couture, Pigott rails against the recent fashionability of certain varietals, especially Sauvignon Blanc and Moscato, which he sees being industrialized to mass-produce uninteresting, homogenous 'identikit' wines. Chardonnay, of course, is the poster child for trendy tipples, and is specially reserved—no pun, winos—for a proper prescription of Pigott pique. He has invented the subcategory 'Bullshit Chardonnay' to describe wines that mask the grape's inherent blandness by the addition of concentrated juice from other, better-smelling grapes.

As The Pope of Riesling (Pigott's other sobriquet) points out, not only is Riesling the most pleasantly perfumed of grapes, the most adroit of grapes and the most food-friendly of grapes, it remains the most affordable in terms of a price/quality balance. Although you can bust a billfold for the really aristocratic stuff, the amount of remarkable Riesling available for under twenty dollars puts it into a whole different value grid than, perhaps, the rarified swank of lone-variety Burgundies or those expensive and exclusive 100% Syrah Rhônes.

Another fact that impresses Pigott is the relatively recent American excitement over his pet cultivar. Riesling, he says (quoting Nielsen data), has been the fasting growing varietal in the United States for five years running.

"The status of wine overall in America fascinates me," he maintains. "It isn't one of iconic items that most Americans identify with themselves or their nationality, although the growth of wine's U.S. popularity is so exponential that the United States is now the biggest wine consumer in the world."

Describing America's headlong foray into Riesling, Pope Pigott I coins a gung-ho marketing hook—'The United States of Riesling'—to identify a prime production belt that arcs from Finger Lakes in New York through Northern Michigan and to the Pacific Rim, especially Washington's Columbia Valley.

"The production of sensational Riesling has tracked the appreciation of wine overall, and America now boasts Rieslings that are serious competition to those from the grape's European homeland."

Pigott, a.k.a, The Ambassador of Auslese, met Sean O'Keefe—perhaps the area's most vocal Riesling supporter—at *Riesling Rendezvous 2000* in Seattle and was moderately impressed, if not blown out of the tub, by what the twin peninsulas of Leelanau and Old Mission were bottling. And it was O'Keefe, along with Amanda Danielson, who organized the Riesling-centered weekend in Traverse City (July 26 – 28, 2014), hauling The Rajah of Riesling in from the Big Apple (where Pigott now resides, though he's failed to rename it the Big Riesling) and setting him up in the adorable Bijou on the Bay theater to screen his documentary. Which is, let's be honest, not exactly Cannes material, but certainly a fun and educational opportunity to watch Paul 'Mr. Terroir' Grieco say 'fuck' and 'shit' like a giddy tenth-grader in wine venues across the USA.

July 27, 2014: No matter the movie; the intro saved the day: Pigott is entertaining as a public speaker and his witty stage banter was worth the price of admission, and it can be fairly reported that he drops the f-bomb only when necessary, and thence, with all the erudition and charm of a genteel English gentleman.

In any event, it was the other event, the afterglow in a broad tent overlooking the broad bay where one hundred Rieslings from around the globe were presented, that was the bacchanalian clambake we'd all been drooling for. And, let it be said via *moi*—not always the biggest champion of Michigan Rieslings when contrasted on a world stage, finding them frequently too elementary and too immediate—that the samples I tried this evening proved that the state is most assuredly in contemporary contention. The universal exception, as always, were wines from the classic estates of the Rhine, Nahe and the Mosel, whose spectacular selections remain undisputed evidence of the ultimate supremacy of German Riesling. Sweet or dry, the examples here exhibited a character that I can only describe in metaphor: It's like the bottom of the tasting glass dropped out to reveal a hidden kingdom of peregrine flavors, some obvious and some subtle, and you are left with a sudden, shimmering revelation that you've confronted an actual landscape rather than a sketchbook drawing.

As it happens, although 100 wines were offered, sanity restricted me to fewer, and the following brief descriptions are a handful of those that stood out.

And please don't say it: Yes, they were cherry-picked.

Ste. Michelle 'Eroica', Columbia Valley, 2012: The first five vintages of this wine made the Wine Spectator Top 100 list, and it remains a benchmark for West Coast Riesling. Bright and peachy, the nascent alpha-numerical terpenes that give riesling a peculiar—and I think, delightful—*je ne sais quoi* overtone of latex—are there, along with a well-rounded stab of acidity.

Black Star Farms 'Tribute', OMP, 2011: The titular 'tribute' is to the 56-acre Montague Estate Vineyard on the Old Mission Peninsula, and the wine shows a soft profile; a precise, detailed and clearly focused blend of grapefruit, lime zest, apricot and clean stone.

Strub Niersteiner Paterberg Spätlese, Rheinhessen, 2013: A mouth-coating explosion of peach jam and lemony tea, the wine slides effortlessly to a crisp and juicy finish.

Reichsgraf von Kesselstatt Piesporter Goldtröpfchen Kabinett, Mosel, 2009: Arguably the most famous vineyard in the Mosel, this five-year-old beauty is just starting to release the intensified aromas of age, including kerosene and honey-rich apricot cream. The sophistication and scope of this relatively inexpensive Riesling is a tough act to follow.

O'Mission, OMP, 2013: An example of a light, friendly Riesling meant to be drunk virtually the same day as it is bottled. An orange sherbet nose and a sweet, Juicy Fruit body, the wine is shored up by Old Mission acidity but doesn't reach any heights of iconography—nor does it aspire to.

Pacific Rim, Yakima, 2013: A Pigott favorite, the wine displays moderate spice—especially mint and tarragon—and a wallop of stone fruit.

Chateau Grand Traverse Lot 49, Molly Devine, 2013: One of the few Michigan Rieslings that achieves consistent heights of intensity, Lot 49 is not a CVS Riesling, and as such, must be approached with the understanding that some of the most sought-after Riesling aromatics (specifically, the 32-letter terpene abbreviated as TDN) take time to develop. When consumed young, these specifically-crafted wines may show as somewhat uninteresting; CGT winemaker Sean O'Keefe has sufficient balls to produce such an interpretation, and as expected, although chomping at the bit to express itself, the 2013 only hints at its potential.

Smith-Madrone, Spring Mountain, 2013: I consider this the top California Riesling, but that is hardly a huge leap—most California vineyards are too low in elevation and too warm for the grape to make any enological noise. Even so, the 2013 is not yet showing well on the nose, but has a beautiful green apple and vanilla cream profile with a lovely, rich mouthfeel.

Loosen 'Red Slate', Mosel, 2012: Another German superlative; the elusive descriptor 'minerality' is like Potter Stewart's famous quote about pornography: *'I may not be able to define it, but I know it when I see it'.* Or in this case, taste it. The slate soils of Erden and Ürzig in the Middle Mosel impart a dense, muscular, mouthwatering sense of stones and clean soil to the wine, dominating, but not masking an herbal headiness and a creamy spiciness.

Konstantin Frank, Finger Lakes, 2012: My top pick for American Rieslings at the tasting, this wine is German in all but appellation, drawing in the unique smokiness, salinity and scents of rainwashed slate of *Das Vaterland*. The Godfather of New York Riesling, Frank first realized that it was the rootstock, not the climate, that accounted for the failure of Riesling in Finger Lakes, and his family has been producing award-winners since 1962.

Shady Lane Cellars, 2012: Adam Satchwell nails it to the wall with his floral, semi-dry Riesling which dances with minerality while providing a rich, creamy wine which makes a concerted effort to restrain the stone fruit profile in favor of more exotic aromatics. Satchwell is somewhat unique as a California winemaker who came here, tried to avoid the Riesling bug, and then was bitten nonetheless following a series of *ah-ha* moments.

I saved Satchwell's Riesling for last, because in his own tasting notes, Stuart Pigott states (emphatically) that this is the best wine that Adam has ever made. And congratulates him! Which is great press for Shady Lane, except for the part when Pigott maintains 'surprise' in the quality of the bevvie. Now, hang on a sec—*surprise??* Isn't he in town to help celebrate Traverse City's newfound position as City of Riesling? Isn't he sitting at a card table in Horizon signing books, winning friends and influencing drinkers? Why surprise? Is he surprised at my surprise at his surprise?

July 28, 2014: Anyway, that brings us around full circle to the saddest circumstance for a writer on Planet Riesling—or any other planet in the contiguous solar system—and it is not trying to sell books to tourists. No, it is the snub suffered by your humble narrator in trying to give— not sell, pawn or haggle a trade for—a copy of his own small sortie into scrolldom (*A Rite Of Paso: Paso Robles Wine Country*, 2013) to Mr. Riesling, the Pope of Potables, the Prince of Piesporter, the Gerent of Johannisberger—Stuart Pigott.

Three times, mind you, I handed him a copy of my book and never once did the gesture of bonhomie amongst those of us who find ourselves as lonely fellows upon this haunted wayside of scribal wilderness wind up with him actually putting a copy inside his goddamn valise, or whatever it is that British German New Yorkers call that silly man-purse.

Thrice! I don't know what they call three-in-a-row in the City of Riesling, but I know what we call it in the Motor City: A hat trick.

And that is the saddest circumstance a writer could face: The literary equivalent of standing on Cass and Selden in a hot little zebra-print mini with a man-purse filled with Riesling-flavored crack, unable to give it away.

GRAND TRAVERSE DISTILLERY GIVES IT THEIR BEST SHOT

It's an interesting question in any case: Does appellation play the same role—or any role—in defining a liquor's quality as it does a wine's?

Or is it purely marketing schtick?

I ask because a wine's regulated place-of-origin is intimately woven with information about that wine's terroir, whether it is as specific as the twenty-acre vineyard of Le Montrachet or all-encompassing appellations like 'California'. With the former, you are legally assured that the grapes in the bottle are Chardonnay, grown in a tiny, mystical plot of land in Burgundy's Côte de Beaune. With the latter, according to the law, a quarter of the grapes don't even have to come from California, and those that do can be grown anywhere in the state; and as a result are likely to originate in the hot, flat, cheap Central Valley. The beautiful thing about this system is that the retail prices of each tend to reflect the exclusivity of the appellation. A California label will likely cost you under ten dollars; a Montrachet, more than five hundred. Whether or not you get what you pay for is a subjective thing, of course—but for the most part, you do.

Landis Rabish of Grand Traverse Distillery told me, with evident pride, that he buys as much grain as he can from Michigan farmers; the only stuff he brings in is the stuff he can't get in any great quantity, like malted rye and barley suitable for whiskey mash. But it can be argued that winemaking is a process while distilling is an art, and how much the raw material has to do with what ends up in your pony glass has little to do with terroir.

Those with better palates than I may disagree, but I'd welcome the chance for them to prove it.

In the case of Grand Traverse Distillery, the bragging rights to Michigan produce is as much an heirloom crow as a nod to eat/drink locovores; the Rabish family has been growing grain and making moonshine since Prohibition. Landis' great-grandfather George Rabish used to distill the excess crop from his Standish farm back in the thirties—some of his equipment, though not used, is still around.

"A lot of the best stuff was tossed out, though," Landis says; the regret in his voice is obvious. "My grandmother didn't like the association with our family and moonshine. We lost a few antique whiskey jugs in the purge that I'd love to get my hands on right now.

Note to Grandmother: You can extinguish the fire, but not the desire.

In fact, distilling seems to have skipped a generation. It was Landis' father Kent, with a background in biology and chemistry, who happened on an artisan vodka maker a decade ago and figured he could match wits with that sort of end game. A whole lot of expensive copper later, he distilled a couple barrels of neutral alcohol made with grain grown by the Send Brothers in Williamsburg and water from Lake Michigan. That became 'True North Vodka', the distillery's flagship spirit, which Landis maintains is distilled 37 times for ultimate purity.

More on 'number of times distilled'—which is, in many ways, a marketing hook—in a bit.

The distillery's growth trajectory was exponential as befits Kent Rabish's background as a sales executive for the pharmaceutical industry. The second year, they quadrupled output to eight barrels (in quantity; vodka is not 'barreled'); the next year saw 15, and this year, according to Rabish, the goal in a couple of years is to produce 250 barrels of liquor—the equivalent of 62,000 fifths, making them the largest micro-distiller in Michigan.

'Large micro-distiller', of course, is an outrageous oxymoron.

Not everything Grand Traverse Distillery makes is vodka, of course—far from it. The Rabish rabble seems to have as much, or more fascination with the browns, and produce a number of interesting variations on the whisky theme, including bourbon.

For the record, bourbon is defined as grain alcohol potted in new, charred, white oak barrels and aged at least two years; of the grains, the law require that least 51% be corn. The rest can be made up of rye, sometimes wheat, and malted barley, which has enzymes that break down starch chains to fermentable sugars. Bourbon is a uniquely American product; to be called such, it has to be born in the U.S.A. The association with Kentucky is largely romantic because Bourbon County, KY—which once encompassed about half the state—can claim to be the origin of the name.

A good thing, because the Rabish regiment wants to keep the home team front and center in the beverage, claiming a 'mash bill' of mostly Michigan agriculture. The bourbon itself is sensational; softly spicy with notes of orange, vanilla and warm caramel; an additional year on new oak, above and beyond the call of duty and not required by law, adds an undertone of smoky charcoal.

The intriguing element of spice in the bourbon is likely the result of the rye content; according to Landis, rye is the traditional distillate of Colonial America, and for many years, Allegheny County, PA was the epicenter of rye production in the United States, accounting for a half-barrel of yearly production for every person in the country. Rye itself is a pedigreed grain, having been favored in Neolithic times, although Pliny the Elder wrote in 70 BC that rye is 'a very poor food and only serves to avert starvation.' Maybe so, but mashed, brewed and distilled, it produces a dry, spicy, fruity liquor that has more of a bite than bourbon and less of bourbon's characteristic sweetness. Rye production the United States died out after Prohibition; popular tastes moved toward the brown sugar, caramel allure of corn-based bourbon. Not only that, says Landis, rye is pricey; he pays 50¢ a pound for rye; less than 15¢ for corn. But for those that love the unique nip of heat and rustic richness that only rye can impart, no other hooch comes close.

Rabish's rye is called 'Old George' after his granddad; it's not only an homage to him, but to old-timers of any designation who made rye before Prohibition. Bottled straight from the barrel without filtering, the unique rye flavors are perfectly represented—nosing a glass is like walking into a room where a loaf of rye bread is baking. There are provocative overtones of allspice and cinnamon and a complex floral that a basic bourbon can't touch. This is a booze for an experienced and experimental palate, perhaps, but part of the learning curve to appreciating liquor—who liked their first snort of Scotch, anyway?—is branching out from the familiar.

Take gin as an example. This botanical brew of juniper and other aromatic herbs, fruits and spices has been popular since the Middle Ages, and because of the variety of possible recipes, many of these are kept under lock and key by those who create a 'house blend'. Most commonly (other than juniper; gin's predominate flavoring), additions include anise, cinnamon, almond, citrus peel, coriander, grains of paradise and nutmeg. The concoctions are only as limited as the gin maker's imagination and they may spend years perfecting the recipe. Landis Rabish has not spent years ruminating (no pun; it isn't rum), but he's definitely spent a whole lot of months mixing and matching, and more than likely, he isn't done yet. The one I sampled had been aged in white oak barrels and showed a slithery softness infused with a myriad of exotic high notes. One of his 'secrets' which is happy to share is that the neutral spirit (wheat vodka) upon which his gin is based is of the highest quality; many producers are less concerned with the purity of the base booze, believing that the botanicals will mask them or the cocktail will, since gin is one of the few spirits that is made to be mixed, rather than consumed straight. Unfortunately, 'GIGO' is as true for distillers as it for computer techs.

In fact, all of Rabish's liquor is built upon the purest, cleanest of foundational spirits—one of the things that he says the multiple distillation process insures.

So, back to that...

When broken down to its most basic elements, the distilling process takes a fermented mash (called a 'wash) and heats it to the several boiling points of the various liquids contained within. Water boils at 212 °F, while ethanol (the pure stuff) evaporates at 173 °F, so in a perfect world, the process should be as basic as heating the wash to the second temperature and re-condensing the steam. Problem is, the organic mechanics of fermentation produces a number of compounds other than ethanol; a few are noxious and some are toxic, and some have lower boiling points than ethanol, and so, are contained within the first 'run'. Essentially, these are poured off, but some remain behind, and to rid the final product of them, you re-distill. In theory, the more times you distill a wash, the purer it becomes. But again, the world is not perfect, and along with some of the bad-news congeners exist some of the flavor volatiles, so a careful balance between what you keep and what you toss out is vital.

Vodka, by its nature and legal definition ('neutral spirit') is on a Holy Grail quest for purity; whiskey, on the other hand, depends on heavier elements for complexity and depth. Rabish's '37-times distilled' brag is the result of his column still (as opposed to a 'pot' still used in Scotch and Irish whiskey production). A column still has a number of plates, each acting as individual pot stills within a tube; the column is heated from the bottom and vaporizes the volatiles with the wash, which rise to the top (where it's cooler) and condense against the plates and shed more of the non-ethanol every time they do. Vodka may be distilled until it is 190 proof, or 95% pure alcohol. Bourbon and rye, which also use the column still method, get held at 160 proof or less.

Essentially, the '37 times distilled' tag-line results from counting the plates and the number of times the vodka has undergone the downward trickle. Even the most exceptionally 'clean' commercial vodkas like Italy's 'Purus' claim quintuple distillation, so at some point, it becomes obvious that number of distillations is more marketing doublespeak than quality indicator. Which is fine—Landis Rabish has a degree in Communications and plenty of retail sales experience to shore up his right to use catchphrases as long as his products lives up to the hype.

And it does. Rabish (and his father) is a true craftsman, which means that no corners are cut and the quest for perfection is ongoing. To me, it matters far less how many times they distill their vodka and even less than that they buy raw grain from Michigan instead of Wisconsin, where they may in fact grow better rye than we do in the first place. What matters is that Grand Traverse Distillery processes, ferments and distills on premise.

Because, far more nefarious to the reputation of micro-distilleries in 2014 are those that do not—despite frequent claims to the contrary—actually distill all their own liquor. As much as 75% of small-batch labels may be marketed and sold by someone other than the distiller for any number of reasons, the most logical of which is that it costs a boatload of cash to open a distillery. Whiskey requires aging, and unless you have very deep pockets or a ready market for fresh vodka, the lag time between the start of production and the release of a brand may be years and years. A new distillery needs cash flow in the meantime, and often those without the slow-growth mentality of Grand Traverse Distillery solve the issue by purchasing bulk whiskey that may not even have been made in the state where it is bottled.

Worst thing? Consumers don't seem to mind.

I do, though—to me, that's misrepresentation.

And because I think so, I'll name names: A single distiller in Lawrenceburg, Indiana called MGPI makes rye distillate for George Dickel, Redemption, Angel's Envy and Smooth Ambler among many others. And not custom stuff, either—it's the very same rye whiskey in every bottle. The logo is the only difference.

In my book, the true art of micro-distilling happens on premise, within the same bricks-and-mortar that bottles it, preferably by the person who pours you a glass in the tasting room. Like Landis Rabish does in his Traverse City oxymoron, Michigan's biggest micro-distillery.

Talk about purity of spirits all you want; that level of purity is one of the essential spirit—the soul—and it outstrips 37-times-distilled every time.

Mike Beck:
The Apple Of My Hich

'If Eve sold her soul for an apple, it's hard to imagine what she'd have given up for a gallon of Uncle John's 'Melded'.'

Shake hands with Mike Beck and you wonder why he needs an apple press at all. He's not just big, he's defensive tackle big—his hands are the size of RV hub caps and look as powerful as any Kreuzmayr fruit mill; given a pot of strong black coffee and a truckload of Ida Reds, I have no doubt he'd do a John Henry on them before the noontime whistle blew.

With a sort of serene potency simmering beneath his titanic surface, Mike Beck has the whole gentle-giant Hoss Cartwright thing going on, but along with the brawn comes the brains, and it's soon apparent that Beck—a fifth generation cider man—has thought about apple wine as much as apple wine can be thought about. And the results may well redefine the way you think about apple wine too.

They did me.

To begin with, there is no enological difference between hard cider and apple wine—the two terms are simply colloquial or legal semantics— TTB regulations require cider to have an alcohol-by-volume of 7% or less, while to legally be considered wine, fermented apple juice must have more that 7% ABV (but less than 24%). Since apples do not naturally reach anywhere near the sugar concentrations of grapes, and since alcohol is a by-product of yeast after it eats sugar (the more sugar it eats, the more alcohol it produces), most un-chaptalized or non-fortified ciders will ferment out in the 5% to 7% range—a punch that is closer to beer than wine.

And that is fine by Mike Beck—his hard ciders hover beautifully around the legally prescribed ABV; they contain nothing artificial and show an array of characteristics unique to a stand-alone variety or as part of a blend. And when it comes to his only product that wears the word 'wine' on the label, his 14% ABV Apple Dessert Wine, it owes its extra octane to apple brandy, distilled on premise by Mike.

That said, citing cider as a 'beer alternative' makes Mike scoff—in his world, that's sacrilege. As proof, he holds his massive palms in an upward cup, saying, "Imagine I am holding apples in one hand, a bunch of barley in the other. Which juice would you rather drink?"

Hard to argue the answer even if you wanted to. Which you don't.

The 'Uncle John' in Uncle John's is Mike's father; he bought the wholesale produce farm from his own parents in the early 1970s and first conceived the value in 'agritainment'—combining produce with a fun day out for Mom, Dad, Buddy and Sis—when the market went a little south. John Beck began by adding doughnut sales to the cider mill and evolved the idea into weekend entertainment acts, seasonal festivals with a whole lot of rip-roaring events in between. So many of the original John's nieces and nephews went to work at the fun farm that the nickname 'Uncle John' stuck.

Where does hard cider and apple brandy fit into that family-friendly formula? In a whole different building, of course.

The farm currently sprawls across three hundred acres, of which about eighty are planted to apples, and it was in the tasting room at the Fruit House Cidery, overlooking those trees, that I first had my pint-sized hand shaken by Mike Beck's prodigious paw.

I don't know it he displays the same passion when talking about the asparagus that he likewise grows, but when it comes to chatting cider, his eyes shine like the apple sitting on teacher's desk in those iconic clip-art illustrations. His pomaceous prowess is astonishing; he has experimented with nearly every sort of heirloom apple you can imagine, helped revive varieties like the Golden Russet—whose rough, potato-like skin makes it unpopular in US grocery stores—and developed cider blends that put him in the forefront of most discussions of the bevvie's revival.

It's called a 'revival', of course, because cider was the most popular drink in pre-Revolutionary America, where water was unsafe and beer barley was difficult to grow.

"The importance of cider to our founding fathers is actually immeasurable," Beck explains. "Entire political platforms were based on it. It was the favorite drink of colonists because it could be made with little technology and with readily available fruit. Beer and spirits required specialized equipment, heat energy and hard-to-source raw products."

In fact, I nurture a fond little personal theory postulating that our very nation's foundation owes itself to hard drink intake. In 1790, United States government figures showed that annual per-capita alcohol consumption for everybody over fifteen amounted to thirty-four gallons of beer and cider, five gallons of distilled spirits and one gallon of wine. That pretty much means that all adults and most teenagers operated on a low-grade buzz from dawn to dusk. Now, suppose you were sitting around with a bunch of friends and colleagues and up came the question: *"Should we—a bunch of struggling colonies without a navy or organized military force—declare war on the most powerful army in the world?"*

What single variable can you imagine adding to equation that would make the answer come up 'Yes'?

Bingo.

Actually, to be won over to the glories of apple wine, there is one cardinal rule that you will need to understand: It isn't grape wine.

By this I mean, it does not have the full-flavored concentration of many of the white wines you're familiar with; ciders are graceful, insinuating and beguiling beverages, alluring in their delicacy. Tannins are softer; bouquets are seductive, subtle and tentative; mouthfeel is bright and refreshing—cider is often effervescent, with flavors that

are fresh and quick to dissipate.

Understand that, and you can approach a tasting with a fair overview of what to expect and not be disappointed by the transience—even brevity—of cider's sensory experience.

We began with his line of cider-in-a-can, a year-round Uncle John's offering concocted from apples like Northern Spy and Jonathan, which have a longer shelf life than the delicate seasonal apples he prefers for his higher-end ciders. It's a simple and refreshing thirst-quencher gone in search of an entry-level cider market. Mike tells me that the entire operation to can 16 ounces of cider costs less than the label on one of his bottles.

These are his pot-boiler ciders; the bill payers.

Stuff starts getting serious with Uncle John's 'Baldwin'—a crisp, mineral-laden cider made entirely with the eponymous fruit—once the leading dessert apple grown in the United States. A severe freeze in the nineteenth century killed off a large portion of American Baldwin trees, allowing the emergence of cold-hardy Macintosh, but Mike believes that as a stand-alone, Baldwin is the superior variety, offering a striking, slate-like character to cider that emerges only when the apple is fermented completely dry.

'Russet', from the ugly apple that the fruit stand can't sell, is a complex, honey-perfumed cider with a rich, earthy palate and a slightly smoky undertow. Russets tend to be sweeter than other golden-skinned apples, and develop aromatics in cold storage, suggesting a water permeability to the russeted skin, leading to dehydration and a greater intensity of polyphenol molecules.

The most visually striking cider in the Uncle John lineup is the limited-edition 'Rosé', made from several rare, red-fleshed apples including Geneva, Redfield and the Asian jawbreaker Niedswetzkyana. It is a beautiful deep pink in the glass, touched with light floral scents and soft apple flavors behind a prickle of effervescence and acidity.

"But the best cider comes from blends," Mike maintains. "And some of the varieties we're raising from the dead are indispensable components in our ciders."

He's gradually planting more European varieties—a difficult process as he experiments with American root stocks (Gala is a favorite) to suit the variety of soils on his acreage, ranging from beach sand to heavy clay. It's always, he says, a crap shoot: Dabinett has adapted well to Michigan's rising damp he claims; Kingston Black—a variety he loves—has not.

Most of his unique apples (Winter Banana, for example, is a beautiful, golden-skinned apple that offers cider a unique aroma that Beck describes as 'daisy' and strikes other as 'ripe banana'; hence, the name) along with standby you-pick-it orchard varieties like Winesap, Golden Delicious, Jonathan and Cortland, find their way into Beck's twin distilling projects. First, apple vodka, distilled as a neutral spirit, is a cool, crystalline-clear sip, only slightly reminiscent of apples and only when you know in advance what it is made of—then, remarkably, it becomes a clear indication of the source. Beck sells it as a satiny stand-alone, and also uses it to fortify his dessert wine—essentially, hard cider with the proof punched up.

His apple brandy requires a bit more time and finesse; it's a well-crafted and rustic eau-de-vie, aged in French oak and one to give Calvados a reason to sit up and take note. It's fierce and floral and long on the palate with hazelnut, toffee, green apple and citrus sliding in tandem from the glass.

Speaking of Tandem, although Uncle John's Cidery is near Lansing, hundreds of miles from Traverse City, Mike Beck warrants this chapter based on his mentorship of Northern cider makers like Dan Young of Tandem Ciders. In fact, in Leelanau and Old Mission, it is virtually impossible to find a cider maker up here who didn't learn their chops from Mike, including—or especially—the best of them.

That, by Mike Beck's reckoning, is Dan Young's 'Pretty Penny', Jay Briggs' (of 45 North) 'Heirloom' and Bryan Ulbrich's 'Relic'. To a man, these ciders display the Beck signature: Bold dryness, charming effervescence and clarity of orchard flavors.

In fact, by a timely gift tossed me by the Cider Gods, when I contacted Ulbrich for a Mike Beck sound bite, the two were together, noodling over the Relic blend for 2014.

Ulbrich, maker of such iconic Traverse City wines as 'Missing Spire' and Riesling-based 'Prose', caught the cider bug a few years ago when Beck came to town and infected everybody.

"It's actually sort of amazing to be in the room with him, " Bryan says. "His understanding of cider making is that intense, that encompassing. I'd been making apple wine for years before I met him; the year did, I made five gallons of cider based on his advice. This year, I'll make 18,000 gallons of cider, based on a lot of the same advice."

I called Ulbrich the next day to learn the outcome of the brainstorming session, and for 2014's Relic, he'll use about 30% Winesap—an aromatic, acidic fruit with a good sugar content—20% Baldwin—his 'backbone' apple for structure and depth—and the rest divided between York, sweet Grime's Golden and a favorite, rare apple among cider makers who vie for the limited crop grown in Buchanan, Michigan, Arkansas Black.

"The right tannin level is always the brass ring for cider maker, and Arkansas Black seems to add this element to the blend better than most varieties. I'd use more if I could get them, but then again, so would everybody else."

...Just as everybody would use more of Mike Beck's *malus aforethought* if they could get it—he is, after all, Michigan's Sultan of Cider, the Pope of the Pomme.

But with his own mill running in overdrive, a quarter million guests passing through Uncle John's each year, fifty thousand gallons of his own cider to make, his massive mitts are full.

LEELANAU PENINSULA: HALFWAY BETWEEN THE NORTH POLE AND TIMBUKTU

On a verdant curve along pretty M22, about halfway up the Leelanau Peninsula, a peculiar landmark stands. It's unique compared to the other 'Scenic Turnoffs' that exist on virtually every promontory overlooking Grand Traverse Bay or Lake Michigan, because there is only one.

It's a sign announcing that you are standing directly on the 45th parallel.

Families pose here; passing drivers may ponder the metaphysical mysteries of space and time; geeks pause to consider the significance of other wine regions that also exist along the same parallel: Bordeaux, Côtes du Rhône, Piedmont, the Willamette Valley.

But the sign—and subsequent photo ops—have nothing to do with wine. It's there because the 45th Parallel is precisely at the midway point between the Equator and the North Pole. Standing there, you are in the middle of everything, dead center in the Northern Hemisphere, as far from Santa as you are from Volcán Cayambe.

In other words, having your grinning mug photographed here is a huge celebration of mediocrity.

The towns that dot Leelanau also celebrate a form of mid-American mediocrity with varying degrees of success. Some cater to the pocket wampum of itinerant tourists; others are content to wallow in Smallville inertia; others remain in a time capsule from an era before the American Dream became infected with night terrors like ebola, sub-prime lending and Justin Bieber.

In Cedar—a slow-paced intersection village about midway up and midway through the middle ground of Leelanau Peninsula, I sat in a tavern for a long time, getting fried on a Friday while waiting for My Man Friday—winemaker Chris Guest—who never showed up. It was hardly time wasted; I love these little georgic Michigan bars, scarved with Christmas lights in mid-July and smelling eternally of old pine and damp cardboard, where you walk in, look around, see a half dozen people that you've never met but who you know without asking were here yesterday, same time, same bar stool, and will be here tomorrow, in the identical spot, as reliable as cold cesium atomic clocks, drinking the same Coors Lights in the same camo hats and Polish flag t-shirts and VFA jackets and having some variation on the same conversation about sports, deer hunting or the Michigan Lotto.

The Lotto is huge in small-town taverns like this. On the day I cooled my heels and soaked my sorrows waiting for Chris Guest, the monitor was poised for a drawing of the Michigan Megamillion, which was then up to $225 mil. People with tickets in hand were discussing their numbers as if the lottery were a game of skill; truth is, not one of them—and you know this again, without asking—would emerge from such a financial windfall emotionally stable. Not one of them *really* wants anything more for tomorrow than what they have today—a barstool and a cold beer at one o'clock in the afternoon beneath a pine wall in an obscure corner of Podunkia, halfway between the North Pole and Timbuktu— except for maybe a chance to leave something to the grandkids.

On the other end of the Peninsula, Northport is showing more ambition, but its renaissance is recent and it is (perhaps) no less a toss of the dice. And, bizarre as it seems, the Land's End of Leelanau—a tiny harbor town at the tip of the tundra where even the trees are stunted—owes its 21st century revival to toilets—at least, to a $12 million sewage treatment system installed in 2008 and turned on the following year.

For a town that for a hundred sixty years had prided itself on a serene milieu of natural beauty, few indignities could have been worse than the Michigan Department of Environmental Quality's 2007 finding that it was leaking sewage into paradise. See, after the Leelanau Memorial

Hospital closed in 2004 and 150 people (in a town of 500) lost their jobs and homegrown revenue streams essentially evaporated, a postcard-pretty environment was all many of the townsfolk figured they had left. Neither was that irony lost on those who knew the history of the bitsy burg, which had been established as a pristine outpost to which wealthy people could escape during Michigan's 1848 smallpox epidemic.

The DEQ's declaration all but mandated the construction of a new, horrifically expensive public waste water treatment system, and a maelstrom of political infighting and negative publicity followed. Inevitably, however, the town's survival won out and a subsidized loan from the state along with individual assessments and monthly fees hustled the pretty little outpost—sometimes kicking and screaming—into the new century.

Amid the requisite storefront boutiques with hand-lettered signs in curlicue cursive, rehabbed historical houses and salons with pun names like Shear Pleasure, Northport Brewing is among the most prominent symbols of Northport's rise from the slop-flavored ashes. Founded this year by Scott and Pamela Cain—a Chicago couple who 'used to 'summer' in Leelanau'—the nano-brewery seeks to capture the essence of the Great Green North by using Leelanau hops and malt from Pilot, southwest of Grand Rapids, the only malt-house in Michigan.

Despite using the noun 'summer' as an excruciatingly blue-blooded verb, the Cains did not start the venture with a family fortune; they employed a rather plebeian crowd-funding platform called Kickstarter to cover start-up expenses and tweak the business plan.

"It was a great way to get in touch with local expectations," Pamela Cain maintains, admitting that the couple is still 'working on meeting all the things our users signed up for'.

"It's a very work-intensive, but fulfilling process," she smiles.

She also chimes in on the town's favorite theme; wastewater management. Without the plant—so impressive that it offers tours—even a glorified homebrew operation producing a couple hundred barrels a year would be impossible.

Keeping the doors open at one of the town's most popular dives, Woody's Settling Inn, had already proven to be so—owners of the once-nicknamed 'Hotel Liquor' held out as long as they could, but having to pump out their holding tanks several times a week ultimately proved an insurmountable expense. The new wave of construction, including Tucker's of Northport, a family dining and entertainment center that fills the hole that Woody's left, Bruce Viger's urban-chic Garage Bar & Grill and a new, but already vital income-generating street festival called 'Leelanau Uncaged' would never have happened without the sewer system, and there is little doubt that the only reason that the now flush Northport City Council did not rename the village 'Flushing' is because Michigan already has one.

Michigan only has one Sutton's Bay, but you could probably beam it up and set it down anywhere in the state and it would hold its own, tourist-wise. This is a town that is not content to be a seasonal retirement village, although it handles that end of the equation well; it has the only movie theater in the county, and for an outsider passing through, it seems to be a template for the municipal aspirations of the entire peninsula—a fusion of fun and funky, a paean to both progress and past with one foot in the crushing tun and the other on a hiking path. Sedate older couples stroll arm in arm at dusk; unrepentant hipsters can find their mahi mahi and Italian-made gelato while kids can get their late night pizza at the Roman Wheel. Art shops are a mainstay, and some decent galleries, too—not just starving-artist crafts in nautical or Native American themes. All this with a year-round population of less than 600, Sutton's Bay is not only interesting from nearly every perspective, it's strikingly clean—always a pleasant and lively stop on a long day through wine country.

Then there's the other side of the finger, the one that faces Lake Michigan, called *Michigami* by the Winnebago, who in turn were called the Puants by the French. Where Sutton's Bay seems to strive to be an egalitarian's nirvana, Leland—with exceptions—seems to embody the county's bi-modal extremes, young vs. old, wealthy vs. poor, outsider vs. longtime resident. If Wikipedia's listed population of Leland (2000) is accurate, amid Leelanau's spackle of communities, it's a veritable metropolis; we know that it absorbed many of Good Harbor's residents—a vanished village that sold itself for its lumber in 1924.

But 2010 census figures give the number of Lelanders as 377, and when I called a couple of township offices, I couldn't find a single soul who had the slightest idea of which one was correct. In any case, the value of Leland's location, at the mouth of the Leland River where a natural fish ladder made it a valued fishing ground for Native people, also makes it an ideal launch for tugs, and a commercial fishing industry grew up around the water's edge. Meanwhile, the number of sawmills was growing and a river dam constructed by Antoine Manseau and John Miller in 1854 was large enough to cause three inland lakes to fuse, forming the 600-acre Lake Leelanau. Between commercial fisheries, iron smelters and logging operations, Leland's blue-collar foundation was firmly in place by the turn of the 20th century.

It was around this same time that the town's gorgeous shoreline and proximity to Sleeping Bear Dunes (named 'The Most Beautiful Place in America' by *Good Morning America* in 2012) made it an increasingly popular destination for vacationers and the Midwest's summer-home wealthy. Cashing in on the influx of Chicagoans and Indianapolitans, Jacob Schwarz built the Riverside Inn in 1902, and it remains in operation to this day.

As does the strange and quaint little clot of shanties known as Fishtown—a pet preservation society project established in 2001 to promote (and milk) the town's fishing heritage via a sprawling salted-minnow lure for tourists. It encompasses smokehouses, overhanging docks, fish tugs and charter boats along with art galleries, boutiques and specialty shops in a setting that is deliciously run-down and rustic-chic.

But at the low end of the population scale (377), the social disparities seem glaring. Take age, for example: Of these 377 Lelanders, more are over 80 than are under 20; fully 40% of Leland's residents are over 65. And Leland's income disparity seems even more pronounced, although this is based solely on government-provided data. In November, 2014, Leland's unemployment rate was 8.10%, about two percentage points above the US mean. 'Average' income of households is $71,000, but as many of these households report incomes under $15, 000 as do over $200,000. According to Sperling's 'Best Places To Live', Leland has a cost of living that is 77% higher than the US median; average home price is more than half a million dollars. And yet, in homes that do have children, 49 list themselves as 'female run' while only 32 consider themselves 'male run'.

A similar pattern exists in Suttons Bay, where the average age is 59 and more citizens are over the age of 85 than under 12. A hundred residents consider themselves part of a 'non-family' household, while 88—one in six—live alone. But the median house cost is more in line with income averages and are about half of Leland's: $271,000.

In both communities, however, the public schools outspend US per-student average by around 10% and the classroom pupil/teacher ratio is around 15/1. That's a huge plus to parents with five figure incomes—folks who do not have winter homes in the Dry Tortugas, who live here year round and who still believe that small towns can teach small-town values; people like my AWOL Cedar Tavern drinking buddy Chris Guest, who I finally caught up with.

He says: "Leland's entire school district is contained in a single building, K through 12. As a result, there's a physical link between the grades; a chain of mentorship that begins early and lasts until graduation. Nobody willingly falls through the cracks. As a result, that building becomes as important a center of social involvement as any that exists in the entire township. It's a symbol of the quality of life up here, and it is the single spot that has never failed to make me glad I moved north—nowhere in Leelanau do I feel a stronger sense of small-town connection or a stronger outpouring of community."

INSIDE THE SCATTERBRAIN OF SEAN O'KEEFE

'Scatterbrain' is his word, not mine. Actually, Sean O'Keefe is one of the most singularly focused winemakers in the twin peninsulas. Most vintners up here learn to say Trockenbeerenauslese; Sean learns the entire German language. Most Michigan Riesling producers read books on Rhine cultivation techniques; Sean moves to Germany and lives them. Ask a Riesling fanatic to list their favorite producers, no problem—but Sean actually tracks them down at the source and riddles them with questions.

On the other hand—to Sean's scatterbrain point—when I finally tracked him down, it was after two failed attempts earlier in the summer, one in which he forgot he had other things going on and another when he simply forgot to show up. Even this time, he forgot that he only had an hour before the babysitter had to boogie.

No worries, Scatterbrain—Traverse City's insta-heirloom Franklin restaurant with its salvaged, century-old back bar from a honky-tonk in Marquette, where Chefs Myles Anton and Gabe Rodriguez have managed a fanciful, phenomenal fusion of Northern Michigan standbys and global culinary sensibility, was a fine location to cool my heels.

The table space and view overlooking bustling Front Street in downtown Traverse City was gorgeous; but not so gorgeous as a dive into Sean's private stock of Rieslings while playing Whack-A-Mole with Sean's rapid-fire delivery, scrawling notes so fast that half of what I write is probably wrong anyway.

In any case, from what I can gather, Sean—who grew up in a communal wine swell bigger than Grand Traverse Bay—did not begin his winemaking career intending to be a winemaker. Three reasons for that: First, his father Ed O'Keefe (founder of Chateau Grand Traverse and Old Mission wine in general) already had a winemaker in German-born Bernd Croissant; second, the possibility that Ed, dealing with the economy of the late Eighties might decide to sell the winery was very real.

And third, he sort of preferred beer anyway.

But in the early nineties, as Michigan was beginning to find its stride with Riesling, Ed opted to keep and grow the business, and as such, he convinced his number-two son (firstborn Ed Jr. wears the title CGT President) to travel to Pfalz for some formal wine training. There, Sean apprenticed at Weingut Jakob Pfleger while studying viticulture at the nearby wine school in Neustadt, and from there, to the wine college in Geisenheim.

It was an unexpected awakening for Sean, and, in fact, altered the apocalypse of his future.

"Before reunification," he posits, "German wine had been in the doldrums. Pretty much, only those in the industry knew who were making the good wines, so when I went, I was able to cherry-pick top estates—Georg Breuer, Johannes Leitz, Helmut Dönhoff—to see exactly what they were doing to buck the trend toward bulk-produced, tutti-frutti German wines."

The seventies and eighties saw a huge market for these wines, with Blue Nun and Black Tower (which weren't even made from Riesling) dominating the German import market and selling over two million cases of semi-sweet honeybear drool in the United States every year.

In the meantime, the improvements being made at the Weingut level were largely behind the scenes and employed by winemakers not interested in international mass-marketing. They were moving away from estery yeasts that produced giant, consumer-pandering aromatics (often at the expense of depth) and had begun to pay requisite attention to the can't-neglect details needed in chilly Teutonic wineland to produce top-shelf riesling. In Pfalz—the world's largest Riesling-growing region—this movement was gathering steam just as Sean was arriving, and he saw immediately that the methods and upgraded mindsets that were transforming the makers of elite, terroir-driven Rieslings could be lessons-learned for Northern Michigan.

"The Germans have lapped everyone else on Riesling so many times that I wanted to be on the ground floor of this new wave of production. When I got into the wine business, Northern Michigan had thirty years worth of experience with Riesling whereas German traditions go back five centuries."

Sean describes his winemaking as 'intuitive'—("I spent biochemistry class staring out the window")—as well as realistic: "Thanks to climate change, Germany is dealing with a whole new set of agricultural parameters. They no longer have anything that we'd consider a 'Michigan winter'. A bad year for them is a good year for us."

A new generation of climate combined with a new generation of savvy, resulting in the revolutionary improvements he saw first-hand while working Pfleger fields and cellars. When he returned to Old Mission Peninsula, Sean had banked a keen respect for two seemingly opposing approaches (the balance between which was key): Knowing when to grab the rudder and when to leave nature to take her course.

It turned out that when you followed those precepts, the Riesling that came out the business end of the tank was different than a lot of the Rieslings Michigan was used to producing—and different from what Michiganders were used to drinking.

"A longer time when the fermented wine is left on the lees—first rack's in January—adds a certain savoriness to Riesling. It tends to show more layers and equilibrium and I believe it ages better."

Also, slightly higher pH makes them more susceptible to bacteria, and occasionally, malolactic fermentation kicks in. To many Riesling producers in the United States, malo is viewed as the kiss of death, but the truth is, not everyone insists on a razor-sharp Riesling, and some sniffers find the slightly buttery aromas behind the classic green apple, citrus and wet-stone nose to be an appealing balance. In Alsace, for example, primo producer Zind-Humbrecht takes a somewhat less intransigent view of malolactic fermentation (during which sharp malic acid is transformed to softer lactic acid), allowing the wine to do what it needs to do. Evidence is their 'Calcaire'—a dry malo-Riesling possessed of a startling and delightful velvety texture.

With Sean, any malo is rare and accidental, but neither does he go to chemical means to prevent it—for the most part, the spontaneous onset of malo (rather than the purposeful introduction of *Oenococcus oeni* cultures) tends to happen only in particularly warm vintages where fruit comes in at pH values above 3.2, and Old Mission Peninsula doesn't see too much of that.

The wines for which Sean O'Keefe has earned the respect of such riesling groupies as Stuart Pigott and everywine pro Jancis Robinson originated as experimental batches he launched upon his return from the Pfalz.

'Whole Cluster' Riesling was one of these dress rehearsals, and it became such a long-run hit that Sean occasionally regrets locking himself into the name.

When employed in white wine production, 'whole cluster' pressing is used to minimize the astringency that sometimes leaves a slightly unpleasant bitterness at the end of a wine—this is in part the result of mechanical destemming, which can actually add more woodiness to the wine by the rather aggressive crushing of the stems. With whole cluster pressing, intact bunches are slowly (that's the key word) pressed to extract grape juice, but not stem juice. As the theory goes, by pressing whole clusters in measured, but gentle increments, the berries tend to rupture at the grape end opposite the pedicle (cap stem) and release juice from various physiological zones at different times, and thus, can be controlled. Rarely are the proanthocyanidins in grape stems, seeds and skins detectable in wines which have been whole-cluster pressed.

That's the laws of physics and the science of biology: Organoleptics tell their own story. Sean's Whole Cluster Riesling 2012 fulfills both the promise and the premise—it is soft and supple without any pithy edges; the super-perfumes of other upstate wines are traded for deep scents of citrus, stone and rich, almost creamy peach notes. It is a beautifully structured, many-layered wine and very Prädikatsweiny in an (ironically) dry, but honeyed and caramelized sugar way.

Lot 49 is another of Sean's brainchildren; a subset, he says, of Whole Cluster. From a new, west-facing Old Mission vineyard situated on what geologists refer to as a drumlin, the vines undergo three separate 'sweeps'; about a quarter is picked early, when acids are barbaric, but most is picked around the third week of October when the Brix has risen to the low twenties. Then, a third pass over the vineyard is undertaken in November, when a touch of botrytis may be present. The acidic reserve takes on the concentrated syrup of the late harvest and enjoys, along with the middle three quarters, a long, slow fermentation with plenty of yeast lees contact, adding savory complexity to the wine—actually made from a French Riesling clone, Entav-Inra #49.

"Riesling is no fool's game," Sean explains about Lot 49; "and my goal is always to unify the layers that develop at various stages of the process. I use techniques I learned from my German compatriots, including a primary fermentation in stainless steel, when most of the heat is generated, then a longer, slower hibernation in *stücks*. These are German barrels, oak, oval in shape and holding 300 gallons, so that there is not a lot of contact between wine and wood. This leaves a Riesling which has sacrificed a little fruit for structure; it may taste a bit restrained to people used to the juicy-fruit wines you can smell across the room, but a lot of these have their acid bones sticking out—a lot of them come across as margarita mix masquerading as Riesling."

Indeed, Sean avoids all temptation to produce what he refers to as 'catalogue wines'—wines made from designer yeasts promising specific estery results, flavor-enhancing enzymes, derivatives and fining agents. He is absolutely in tune with his terroir—which is to say, he is honest about its limitations. "In Michigan, grapes don't always ripen uniformly; in 2009, our yields were barely able to skitter over the finish line. We have narrow parameters and I prefer to work within those, and that means no chaptalizing [adding sugar] and not trying to produce quick wines with a lot of up-front, simplistic appeal on release, but which quickly become vampires in the sunlight and die quick deaths. My wines are made to age with grace and become more complex—not less complex—in the years after they are bottled."

It can be a frustrating go, but it's a struggle that all minimalist winemakers face, especially those in wine country where—as happened in the winter of 2013-2014—the lake effect fails as Lake Michigan freezes and a huge portion of the crop succumbs to winter kill.

But in the really fine years, the dividends of Sean O'Keefe's level of dedication and integrity pay off. Take 2010 for example, when all the *je ne sais quoi* combined with all the *sais quoi* and produced a wine so lovely that Jancis Robinson OBE, MW named it her February 10, 2012 *Wine Of The Week.*

Since I dig her writing chops, I'll quote them verbatim:

"I loved the energy in this wine, the slightly funky but extremely interesting nose and the fact that it tasted bone dry (total acidity is 7.8 g/l, pH 3.25) but had such an impressive array of wild-flower aromas. I gave it 17 points out of 20 for what it is worth and would drink it with great pleasure from now for the next five years."

The only downside is that only 130 cases were made, so if you want some, you may be hard pressed (wine pun) to find a bottle at any price.

But, as in all wine endeavors, as Sean O'Keefe's globe-hopping résumé makes obvious, the search for the Grail is half the fun of the journey.

WARREN RAFTSHOL:
PERIPHERAL PERSISTENCE

Whenever I stop in to see old Warren Raftshol in Leelanau's answer to Area 51, I'm sort of overwhelmed; I feel both wildly lonely and strangely optimistic. He hangs on inside his wayward depot despite the odds, and Warren—whose sculpted face is a Dorothea Lange wet dream—greets all comers, new and old, with a sort of fierce, fatalistic indifference.

Asked about his views about the changing visage of Leelanau wine country, he offers exactly that, shrugging, "The wine business is pretty much a blur to me."

Such a response might be viewed by some scribes as interview-kryptonite, but not me—by golly, to me Warren Raftshol is the Grand Traverse lighthouse, still standing and always accounted for despite the ravages of time, the gales of November coming early or juggernaut technology. Like the lighthouse, Warren Raftshol essentially serves the same function as he has always served; and, like visiting the lighthouse, is accompanied by a certain wistful melancholy, a glance at Warren Raftshol's secluded, ramshackle tasting room, where inside, unsold wine sits in cardboard cases and outside a stone silo slowly crumbles to dust, the experience is a snapshot of the flip-side of Leelanau's emergence as an appellation worthy of notice.

The Grand Traverse Lighthouse, incidentally, has been operating since 1857, and although Warren's tenure as a winemaker is less, I wouldn't bet on it being too much less. From what he can remember and from what I can glean from outside sources, the Raftshol family has been a fixture on the peninsula for many generations. A page from the Sutton's Bay High School Class of 1926 yearbook shows Rudolph Raftshol—Warren's uncle—among fifteen graduating seniors; a 2014 edition of *Leelanau Enterprise* notes Olivia Raftshol—Warren's niece—entering the Marines. Within the archives of that same newspaper, Warren's name keeps surfacing with a certain WTF? charm. For example, in a February, 2012 column about Leelanau County's *'Odd and Quirky'*, Warren is described as *'a one-time write-in candidate for Leelanau County sheriff whose political views appear to come from somewhere to the right of Attila the Hun.'* Yet another piece on medical marijuana that same year leads with, 'Finding someone in Leelanau County who will admit publicly that they plan to vote "yes" on Proposal

1 in November is not an easy task,'—then goes on to quote the single yes-voter willing to go on record: Warren Raftshol.

Needless to say, he did not win his sheriff's badge. Nor a bong.

Stories abound about Warren's eccentricities, and most of them are pretty quaint and pretty hilarious, but I won't relate them. Not because I don't want to, but because the people who told me them don't want me to—and I have to respect that. See, around here, Warren Raftshol— if not exactly venerated—is treated like any Historical Marker. Regardless of your opinion over what it represents, you don't leave your cigarette butts on the front lawn.

What Warren Raftshol and his one-man wine show represents is Leelanau wine country as it was in the beginning, ain't now, and likely will never be again.

Like many area winegrowers, the Raftshols began in the tart cherry business, souring on it in the '60s when prices dropped, finally tossing in the red-stained towel in the 1980s after Warren's father passed away and the trees had outlived their productive cycle. By that point, Warren had jobbed himself out as a pruner at Leelanau Wine Cellars in nearby Omena, and had developed a fascination for what grapes could do on land that had formerly been planted to Montmorency and Morello cherries.

Although today he expresses no interest in hybrids, in the early days of wine growing in the peninsula, the Leelanau Fruit Company of Sutton's Bay was advising farmers who wanted to get into the nascent wine biz to go the safe route.

"The co-op was more cautious in those days," Warren relates with a small sneer. "And farmers tended to do what the co-op told them." He cites the lead taken by the pioneers of the Leelanau wine community: "Bernie [Rink], Larry [Mawby] and Bruce [Simpson] all planted hybrids, so that's what I did. I put in Aurora and Chelois; didn't like the wine. Those fields have since been grafted over to Cabernet Franc."

In fact, according to former Raftshol winemaker Chris Guest, one of the props due Warren Raftshol is his dogged persistence of *vinifera* in the peninsula, particularly red grape varieties.

"Peninsula Cellars made a popular blend from Warren's vineyards; Raftshol Red," Guest says. "A mix of everything, Cab Franc, Cab Sauv, Merlot and Pinot Noir. That was not only one of the area's first attempts to promote vineyard-specific bottlings, back when the industry was trying to gain a foothold, those vines were often the first indication to outsiders driving through—a few of 'em lost trying to get to the casino—that the focus of the peninsula was shifting from cherries to grapes."

By his own admission, Warren Raftshol can no longer afford a winemaker. He also (proudly) insists that he stopped chaptalizing his wine in 2008 and one is forced to wonder if he simply can't afford the sugar. While true to variety, his wines are uniformly and sometimes painfully acidic—a teaspoon of sugar would have no doubt helped the Cabernet go down.

Acidic wines, ramshackle winery, unkempt-looking vines, taciturn tasting room host, somewhat creepy photo of Jean Raftshol (1919-2001, Warren's mother) on the label; you'd think this story is, to me, nothing but an endless pejorative.

Not so and not by a long shot: When I stop by Raftshol Vineyards, I do it for the man, not the plan. I do it because he is a reflection of his product: Thin, acidic, ramshackle and somewhat creepy—but, like the lonely lighthouse at the tip of the peninsula, outdated by modernity yet standing strong against opposing tides to mark the passage of Lake Michigan eliding into Grand Traverse Bay, Warren Raftshol remains as an outpost of originality in a sea of increasingly gentrified business models.

GETTING YOUR GOAT AT TC'S BADDEST BODEGA

Long ago and far away, no circumambulation of Northern Michigan wine country was complete without a didactic pit-stop at the odd blue shop wedged between Peninsula Drive and E. Front Street.

There, surrounded by a cornucopia of bottles from distant galaxies like Priorat and Rheinpfalz (as well as the best collection of Michigan wine then available), sat a bespectacled young man whose nose was always stuck in some bizarrely huge wine book; he was a wine nerd extraordinaire, and back then it was sort of fun to pester him with extremely off-the-wall questions, like, "What's the difference between degrees Brix and degrees Plato?" to which he'd always reply, "That's easy," and give you a response so technically convoluted that you wound up being more confused than before.

The fellow's name was Bob Paulinski, and he went on to achieve the nearly impossible feat of becoming a Master of Wine, then sold the shop and went on to do something even harder: He re-invented himself as Sam's Club's corporate wine director, where he grew the chain's private label wines from zero to $82 million in less than five years.

I imagine that to Barefoot Cellars, his tenure at Wal-Mart was what Armageddon is to Christianity.

That was then and this is now, and my first inkling that the Blue Goat might be a new goat was the marquee out front advertising Barefoot Cellars, and a Googled interview with store manager Ryan White contained this quote: "Barefoot is a staple here."

I guess that Barefoot would have been a staple for Paulinski, too: A staple from a Makita pneumatic gun to the *sulcus terminalis* of his tongue.

But like first impressions, first inklings are often wrong, and I after spending half an hour with Ryan White and his dad (who owns the place), I am man enough to do a huge and genuine *mea culpa.*

Maybe nobody on the current Blue Goat staff is passing any Masters of Wine exams any time soon, but of course, since 1953, less than three hundred über-geeks in the visible universe have proven themselves the equal of that task. Today's Blue Goat educational font is the *Wine Spectator School*, an online course that Ryan swears by. And the shelves are stocked with ten thousand excellent bottlings to prove it; the small display of two Barefeet for $11 is easily overlooked.

"We strive to be what I think of as a 'genuine' wine shop; a place that is prepared to hand-sell wine to exactly suit a customer's needs," Ryan says. "I'm willing to spend as much time with a customer as they have to spend."

And it's rare or never that Ryan can't find something that works; The Blue Goat offers the widest selection of wine in Northern Michigan, both domestic and imported, and a pretty hefty beer list as well.

But that brings us to local wine, the star that crowns the Goat. When Paulinski ran the joint, Michigan wine was represented, but area wineries had not nearly reached the apex they have today. Indeed, The Blue Goat has an entire room dedicated to them, and they make up a good 30% of stock keeping units. Ryan points out that his price structure is sometimes better than what you'll find in the various tasting rooms themselves (although the tasting rooms will hope you forget that I just said that). In any case, The Blue Goat is a Michigan wine wish-list with the best from the local best. Back in the day, when Paulinski was noodling *The Wine Economist* behind the register, the state of the art was very much the state of the start-up.

My conclusion?

You don't have to know the difference between Brix and Pluto if your brix and mortar remains true to purpose. Blue Goat is now a blue icon that outstrips its blue-blooded iconhood; even better than before.

And not for nothing, Bob Paulinski is now a Senior Vice President at *BevMo!,* which sells more Barefoot Cellars in an hour than Ryan White does all year.

VERTERRA WINERY
AND MY PERSONAL QUEST FOR JIM
HARRISON

Long ago and far away, when many of you whippersnappers were still drinking wine out of Evenflo baby bottles and I was scarcely old enough to steal vodka from my parents' liquor cabinet, I headed up to the Leelanau Peninsula to search for my then-literary idol, Jim Harrison.

At the time, Mr. Harrison had only published a handful of novels and was still a Northern Michigan landmark instead of a Hollywood wonk-eyesore; inevitable stylistic comparisons were made between him and Hemingway.

Even so, then as now, my reading preferences leaned toward Harrison, and in fact, *Warlock* and *Sundog* were foundations of my fantasy to pursue fiction as an occupation.

My success in that particular venture should be glaring, as you are reading an obscure wine book instead of a *NY Times* bestseller.

Anyway, my quest for Harrison himself bore more fruit. Like any good novel groupie, I'd have loved to have shot the shit with old Ernest, but by the time I was born he'd already left his hypothalamus on the cove molding of his Ketchum foyer. However, I had been assured by the alcoholic intelligentsia that Jim Harrison—a native son of Grayling, Michigan—could be found in a specific Leland bar more nights than not. So up I went, my ticker fluttering and flip-flopping, no doubt expecting that Harrison would embrace some random downstate teenager, take him under his wing, edit, spell check and rewrite heartfelt drivel, set him up with a publisher and find him a local girl.

Hey, it could happen.

Instead (cutting to the chase), I found him in a condition which I believed to be half-tanked (I could be wrong), trying to scam on barfly chicks (I could be wrong), playing an odd billiard game called bank pool (I could be wrong; maybe nine-ball) and received a quick, cursory, courtesy-free brush-off (I'm not wrong).

Bitter?

Seriously? No way: I'm getting mileage out of that story to this day.

What does this have to do with Verterra Winery?

The Bluebird—the bar where this all happened—is owned by the same dude that owns Verterra, Skip Telgard.

In fact, I like to believe that the entire vivacious Verterra venture, which includes Skip's partner Paul Hamelin, winemaker Shannon Walters and consultant Doug Matthies, was conceived right there at the hundred-seat Bluebird bar over a growler of Good Harbor Fishtown White.

But I could be wrong.

However it happened, it happened right; the winery's first vintage won seven medals at the Michigan Wine and Spirits Competition and last month, the next vintage took Pacific Rim Wine Competition's Best In Class for Pinot Blanc 2011 and Chaos White Cuvée 2011—a category that required unanimous 'ayes' from the judges.

To ice that cake, Verterra's Dry Riesling 2011 won a gold medal at the same competition.

Trust me, vineyards that have specialized in riesling for decades aspire to take home gold at the Pacific Rim.

As a Latin contraction, Verterra translates into *'true earth'*—unless, of course, you happen to speak Latin, in which case it really doesn't. More like 'spring earth'.

But, that's no biggie. The Verterra tasting room is the biggie.

Ensconced within a 1927 building shell that originally housed S.R. Gains's tonsorial parlor (Latin for barbershop) and a Jim Harrison-approved pool hall, the short-board maple flooring and funky-looking borrowed-brick exterior has the place oozing the alluvia of D.I.Y. history. Within, manager Jeff pours through the award-winners with expertise and aplomb (Latin for flyness), pointing out, amid his schpiel, that one of the most unique and exciting things about Verterra is that it is family-owned and operated.

Now, that's worth a book in itself, because if me and my family—extended or otherwise—ever opened a winery together, the only exciting part would be the 911 domestic violence calls and the only unique thing about it would be how quickly it closed.

But holding it together quite remarkably is Paul Hamelin, his wife and winemaker son Geoff, crediting (in this order) the custom crush skills of Shannon Walters and the true earth—especially the trio of magnificently productive vineyards from which the winery draws fruit.

Now, anybody who knows Walters' work knows that he could probably make drinkable wine out of the cladophora algae that clogs Grand Traverse Bay, but with the advantage of his solid rep (based on twenty-odd years of vintership in Michigan), he doesn't have to. So impressive is he both as a technician and an artist—he's been called (somewhat belatedly) 'the guy who can finally put Michigan on the world's wine map'—that his skills remain in demand at wineries throughout Leelanau and Old Mission. The fact that he's hauling down medals for each of them—so many that gold no longer seems an element precious enough to do these wines justice—he's maybe into X-Kryptonite territory by now—proves that his purple thumb is pressed with equanimity upon the foreheads of his patrons.

Of course, as Galileo did for the Marchese del Monte and the Grand Duke of Tuscany, as da Vinci did for Cesare Borgia and as Michelangelo did for Lorenzo de' Medici, Verterra's owners initially found their social status improved by Walter's magic-touch wines festooned with ribbons and medals. So maybe that's an exaggeration, but they do get to sit and gloat before wine writers such as I, who may not perch upon the same belletristic throne as Jim Harrison, but whose eyes, at least, track.

So, the last time I stopped by The Bluebird, I noted that nearly the entire staff was too young and ditsy to recognize George Harrison let alone Jim Harrison, so I didn't bother asking.

On the way out, however, I noted a hostess of such profound maturity and gravitas that she probably would have recognized Benjamin Harrison.

So I inquired after the crusty, lazy-eyed poet, sharing my erstwhile pilgrimage to seek him out, to which she replied, 'Oh, back then, lots of young people did...'

Great. Being herded into a category with a thousand other silly little twits with the same goddamn story to tell really made my night. On the other hand, she shared the news that Harrison still stops in when he's in town. Now 77 years old and phlebotomizing gravitas, having proven himself an author able to hold his own against literary giants like Faulkner, he has apparently grown sedate and comfortable in his discerning dotage.

She insisted that he sat quietly and enjoyed a drink-free dinner: A plate of fried whitefish—the house specialty—casting his weird, solitary eyeball toward neither Farmer's Daughter, pool table nor arsenal of booze bottles.

That's what she said, anyway. But she could be wrong.

Guestvin: It's Not Just For Breakfast Anymore

I first met Chris Guest when the two of us were considerably younger men; I was a fledgling wine writer and he owned the only winery in my county. I put in a single harvest with him, picking grapes and watching how he worked the cogs and wheels of winemaking; I was paid via the wine I could swig in the tasting room before and after we started our day.

That unique winery—Seven Lakes Vineyard—produced wines worthy of some of Detroit's top restaurants, placed there by some of Detroit's top sommeliers: Madeline Triffon poured Seven Lakes Vignoles at the London Chop House and Claudia Tyagi did the same thing at The Whitney. Local culinary legends like Brian Polcyn and Ed Janos adored Guest's juice and featured it at trendy Too Chez and Pike Street. Despite this exposure, Guest's labels were (by his own admission) not always top-shelf material, but they were evidence that mid-Michigan could grow drinkable wines far from any western-shore lake affect.

Seven Lakes has long since given up the Guest ghost, but I've maintained contact with Chris over the years, in part because we are kindred literary spirits—he's an excellent poet and from solid stock: His great uncle, Edgar Guest, was not only Poet Laureate of Michigan but was a favorite of Edith Bunker, who often quoted him during *All In The Family*; his sister, Judith Guest, wrote *Ordinary People*. But it's also because the evolution of a winemaker is often as fascinating as the evolution of a writer.

Guest took his baby wine steps with stuff his father made, ten gallons at a time, under the stairs, in a cubby known by the family as 'The Room That Aunt Jean Painted'. Harry Guest owned an envelope factory in Detroit and made wine from California grapes he purchased at the old produce terminal on Fort Street. But one of their neighbors—a horticulturist named Karl Bailey—had planted a plot of hybrid vines on his Troy, Michigan property, proving to the Guests that Oakland County could produce wines not dependent on the *labrusca* workhorse grapes Concord and Niagara. And this spawned a larger plan: Upon retirement, Harry Guest bought a hundred acres of farmland in Holly, about 50 miles north of Detroit. At the time, Chris was playing foot-loose in the warm Caribbean, and when I asked him how his father managed to lure him back from paradise to make wine in the Frost Belt, his reply was unequivocal: "I didn't get the impression that saying 'no' was an option."

So back he came, and together they planted 15 acres of Vignoles, Cascade, De Chaunac and Aurora along with 2500 apple trees, hedging not only the vines but the bet. The first vintages were spotty, the wines came in at varying quality levels and the biggest production year was less than three thousand cases. But the family farm was soon to become a destination place because of Guest's wild tasting parties, complete with outrageous local bands and food. During the fifteen years it was in operation, these weekend shindigs were as much a part of the Seven Lakes legacy as the product.

In any case, the experiment ran its course in the mid-Nineties; Chris had made the best wine he was likely to make given the all the variables, and he began to sniff around Northern Michigan, where he believed the half dozen wineries then in existence were on to something remarkable. He loaded up an old Fiat and headed north, stopping for oil along the way and forgetting to replace the cap, seizing the engine on M37 in Old Mission Peninsula. A fortuitous FUBAR by all accounts, since the guy who bailed him out happened to be buddies with Ed O'Keefe, who was by then making some pretty stand-up *vinifera* at Chateau Grand Traverse. Tasting through O'Keefe's line-up, Guest had his suspicions about the appellations potential confirmed and immediately fired off some letters of introduction.

He wound up being hired by Bruce Simpson at Good Harbor Vineyards.

"Bruce was one of the original believers," says Guest. "He'd been growing cherries up here for years, so he knew the land better than anyone I'd met. But he needed some help with winemaking, and he brought me on board. I thought of it as 'artist meets businessman' arrangement."

From there, Guest went on to make wine for Tony Ciccone in the first couple of Ciccone Vineyard vintages; he made wine for Mike Jacobson at Leelanau Cellars and Warren Raftshol at Raftshol Vineyards, and finally staged his longest-running appearance at Willow Vineyards, where he has been for eleven years.

"John and Jo Crampton have the right idea about winemaking in Leelanau," he maintains. "We've focused on Burgundian varietals, Chardonnay and Pinot Noir, but they've given me the freedom to work with the fruit that we can grow and urged the development of a specific regional styles. We grow Burgundy's grapes, but we don't pretend to make Burgundy. Our Pinot Noir tends to be light in color with a lot of zing and a very recognizable brightness of flavor."

§

Leelanau is Guest's adopted wine country, but he has traversed it as much as any vintner I know. I'm grateful to tap into his intimate grasp of the terroir as we drive around the peninsula in his beat-up (but oil-sated) jalopy. He points out some of the land's striking expressions of lake effect: In early December, some of the inland drumlins are covered in drifts, a couple feet deep in places, while other swaths of ground bear only the lightest dusting of snow. Other properties—entire vineyards, in fact—are still snow-free: *Location, location, location* as a real estate mantra has never held so immediately true.

Of course, in areas where the cold gets particularly severe, snow has an insulating effect, and in sub-zero temperatures, a certain amount of the white is precipitation devoutly to be wished. Guest indicates some newer vines planted in damp valleys where he doubts they'll survive—too low, too wet—and others, older vines, which have all but succumbed during the last season.

But, a wistful touch of disillusionment creeps in around the edges of the screed. Says Guest, "I grew into winemaking reading Alexis Lichine, Maynard Amerine; I was in love with the poetry of wine, which required the attention to detail of any high art. I thought of wine as something holy, something elevated. As a winemaker, reality quickly hits you in the face. You'll always be limited by what you can sell and by the parameters of what your vineyard hands off to you to work with."

That said, the excitement in his voice is unmistakable as we pass a wide, fallow hillside that he believes would be an ideal site for Chardonnay; he wonders who owns it. The fire within, even after numerous harvests with howling polar vortices flung upon it, smolders still.

I got my advice and peninsula tour for the price of a couple of Jack Daniels at some podunk bar that looked like it had been beamed down from Northern Exposure; yours may run a little more. Guest's consulting service, called Guestvin, is available to those with the spirit but not the *savoir-faire*; the passion, but not necessarily the perspicacity of his thirty years of Michigan winemaking.

It's innate understanding by now, but when pressed to distill it into a single, encompassing aphorism, this is what he comes up with:

"Don't make wine like your Dad did in the room under the stairs."

Shannon Walters:
Portable Talent

For a guy who says he doesn't like wine events, Shannon Walters sure seems to show up at a lot of them. Either that, or he is such a remarkable sight that he's the first person you notice when he does. Tall, brutally good-looking with Fabio fringes and a theatrical carriage, he's got a stage presence that rivals any apricot-scarf-wearing diva in

Carly Simon's *'You're So Vain'* and cultivates—by his own admission—an ego big enough to match.

And to his point, whoever the dude might have been in Carly's tune, the song *was* about him.

This song, on the other hand, is about the jumbled set of emotional contradictions that makes Shannon Walters one of the most complicated individuals you can find up here—and that says a lot. He is, perhaps, better than anyone else, a metaphor for the underbelly of Traverse City society, where the haves and have-nots are an almost feudal division of classes and the twain generally prefer not to meet.

Except that, on a small peninsula which has largely devoured most traces of a middle class, meeting each other is sort of hard to avoid.

Shannon came from what in popular parlance it referred to as 'the wrong side of the tracks' and which in Leland may be thought of as the wrong side of Indiana Woods, where houses can range in the low millions. This influx of mostly out-of-state, second-home cash impelled *Forbes Magazine* to refer to the area as 'The new Hamptons', due in part to the fact that New Yorkers can get there—via a two-hour flight from LaGuardia—in less time that it takes them to drive to the real one.

Native to Leland, Shannon was raised in a single-parent home; he dropped out of high school to pursue snow-boarding—Northern Michigan's equivalent of opting out of the rat race to live the life of a Malibu beach bum. To support this unlikely dream, he worked as a cook at Leland's Riverside Inn, where a nascent perfectionism drove him to make 'perfect crispy fried chicken every time'.

That may sound flippant, but it happened that one of his regular crispy chicken customers was Bill Skolnik, then winemaker at Leelanau Cellars, and so impressed was he about this small attention to detail that he offered the teen-aged Walters a cellar rat gig at the winery once tourist season ended. Twenty-two years later, Walters describes what happened next as, "A pretty fucking wild ride."

He'll ask us to pardon his French, but why should we? This is who he is and this is the guy that everybody else begrudges respect: A poor kid from a rich dude's town who the rich folks wind up hiring to make their wine. People who knew him at the outset say he was a rough-and-tumble street kid living a bohemian lifestyle while the scions of wealthy locals (which include names like Ball and Lilly and the fortunes thereof) who were going through a bohemian wannabe stage sort of gravitated to him—he was the real deal.

Turned out that he was the real deal in the wine cellar, too. "I noticed from the beginning that my olfactory senses were unique," he claims. "Then, like now, I could pick up scents in the fermentation tanks that told me certain things were going on. A lot of the time, other, more experienced winemakers didn't notice them. Learning to manipulate those things—fermentation management—is key to how I make wine."

He had an eerie knack for all phases of winemaking in fact; even his detractors give him that much. And there are a few of those, although it can be said in fairness that one of the reasons his detractors detract is his self-diagnosed ADHD, often making him an employee who is hard to track down let alone supervise. Ironically, this is also part of his talent, allowing him to skitter between tasks, vineyard to cellar while still putting a fun and funky face to the public persona of whatever winery's he's representing. And there have been a few; over the years, he's bounced back and forth between new and established wineries like a boho free-spirited hacky sack footbag; whether or not these arrivals and departures were on his own volition depends on who you ask. Whatever the story, he racked up an impressive array of medals and awards in prestigious competitions along the way, and in an era when taking gold in, say, the *2004 Pacific Rim Wine Competition* just wasn't *done* by a Michigan Pinot Gris. But Walters did exactly that during one of two stints at Leelanau Cellars, while helping build it from a middle-of-the-road, fifteen thousand case winery to one that now produces over a hundred thousand cases annually.

Actually, a list of his achievements on the medal front is pretty remarkable, regardless of whether you ultimately feel that wine competitions are legit. In 2011 alone, wines he produced for a trio of wineries (Verterra, Boathouse and Longview) pinned down six gold medals—two of them 'Double Gold'—in five prominent competitions.

Again, on cue, detractors raise heads and hands; the claim made is that Shannon manipulates certain wines *specifically* to win competitions, not grace shop shelves—that he employs specific yeasts that bring out certain early-peaking esters which show at shows, but do not survive the first year in the cellar. The folks who make these claims may or may not have won gold medals of their own, but others—who do not compete—occasionally say that there is a certain 'sameness' to Walters wines, despite different labels, so that a Rosé of Pinot Noir (say) from one winery is indistinguishable from another.

And that's a dis that Walters finds disingenuous, disappointing and disconcerting:

"I'm not sure that's even possible," he says. "In each of these wines, a whole different kinetic goes on. The treatment may be similar, but for the most part, I didn't plant these vineyards, so there are clonal differences, location differences, different densities and spacings; some rosé is grown for that specific end result, others are the result of a cooler growing season. If you think a wine from Verterra tastes like a wine from Boathouse, chances are you may not know as much about terroir as you think you do."

It's a fair rebuttal; although it is equally fair to say that if you are starting up a winery in Northern Michigan, your first year will cost you more than a house on Indiana Woods. So, if this is a business venture, you probably are a lot more fearful of making a shitty wine that no one wants than a cookie-cutter wine that sells.

And at this point, Shannon Walters agrees: "That's why I started One World Winery Consulting. We provide new wineries with everything they need, from concept through to design and completion. If you are going to spend a million dollars to open your doors, you don't want to go in half-assed, because that's what is going to come out the other end."

And the upcoming winter may prove that out, since more than a couple people in Northern Michigan—including Shannon—are already seeing signs that point to another upcoming winter waterloo. With his decades-long experience in managing cold-climate vines, he is filled with schemes and suggestions and snow-scams, and is probably the dude I'd call early to help alleviate a potential cataclysm—many wineries that survived last winter with reserve wine stock, will be out if this winter (no pun) goes south: "If we get hit with another polar vortex—and these things can come as part of a larger pattern, several years in a row—everything above the snowline is toast. Among other things, I'd be laying down renewal canes and managing vines now rather than later."

If worse comes to worse, from a guy who has seen how an infusion of cash into the frosty peninsula can right as many wrongs as it can cause, he shrugs his shoulder toward Old Mission, where the *nellessara* hoop-houses of Villa Mari create a greenhouse environment for grape vines.

"If your pockets are deep enough, and you can spend an extra fifty grand per acre, you'll survive. Of course, your wine winds up costing $50 plus per bottle—sort of unheard of for a Northern Michigan wine— but if you are the last man standing, that becomes the benchmark price, doesn't it?"

One of One World Winery's company catchphrases is, "There's a solution to every problem."

With his Horatio Alger, up-from-the-bootstraps tale of self-determination, even if the solution winds up being a bitter pill for subsistence-level winemakers of Northern Michigan to swallow, be assured that the prescription comes from Shannon Walters having walked the hardscrabble walk.

JUMPING THROUGH HOOPS

The vineyard is shrouded in as much mystery as it is in plastic tents. Calls to the owner go unanswered. Requests for an interview, made through friends, are ignored. Bottles of the wine appear on shop shelves before the winery opens. The goal, ostensibly, is to grow grapes that have no business growing in Old Mission Peninsula because the terroir simply won't support them.

The solution to Villa Mari owner, apparently, is just as simple: Buy the terroir.

Now, that's a remarkable enough goal, befitting a race who can plant flags in the Sea of Tranquility and simulate a breeze for the photo op. This is the brainchild of a species who diverts an entire river to build Los Angeles in a desert, then recreates Rome to make a movie there; these nutty humans have likewise mastered the art of powered flight, run a four minute mile, solved the Poincaré conjecture and made Miley Cyrus a trillionaire. When stacked against the status quo of monumental human achievements, raising drinkable Nebbiolo in Zone 5 (Piedmont is Zone 9) is well within mortal grasp.

As long as you've got the dough-re-mi.

The unreachable star of Villa Mari is owner Marty Lagina, who is also the owner of Heritage Sustainable Energy, a Traverse City alt-energy provider with over 120,000 acres of 'prime' wind developable property in Michigan alone. Heritage's principals have owned or managed conventional energy projects with an aggregate value in excess of $3 billion, so there's the dough. The equation's 're', like Julie Andrews', is a drop of golden sun, since in this northerly latitude, Old Mission Peninsula has more minutes of summertime daylight than any California vineyard.

The 'mi', of course, is unfettered ego. Nothing wrong with that—as the man says, 'Nice work if you can get it.' Marty Lagina likes red wine and claims that he just didn't warm up to the ones grown locally, so with bombastic, Cecil B. DeMille-style overkill, he decided to recreate Rome in the boondocks, including a 15,000 foot cave to hold wine at an optimal, year-round 55°. It's primarily this scale of investment— estimates run between $30,000 and $60,000 per acre for the *nellaserra* infrastructure alone—that make Villa Mari the trophy wife of Northern Michigan wine country.

Of course, the reality-translation of hoops to hootch puts the bottle price of Villa Mari into Everest territory for Northern Michigan. In 2013, 67% of Michigan-made wines sold for between $10 and $20 a bottle; 25% were under $10, and 8% were between $16 and $30. Wines with price tags higher than that didn't even chart. In fact, in 2013, the average price of a bottle of supermarket wine across the entire United States was under $10.

At Villa Mari (which, granted, does not aspire to be a Piggly Wiggly anchor SKU), there is a trio of *nellaserra* wine available:

'Bel Tramonto', a self-styled 'Super Tuscan', made from Merlot and Sangiovese, sells for $39.

'Row 7', another mystery, is labeled as a random blend of grapes from the initial 1999 planting. But that's how Villa Mari wines managed to be available years before the winery opened. Lagina grew grapes long before the hoop houses, and his wine has been made by Sean O'Keefe at nearby Chateau Grand Traverse for the past five years, and Sean has been hired full-time for future releases. Row 7 sells for $49, and on the website, boasts a five-star rating from someone named Dan Misiaszek—which is yet another mystery: The only man with this name that a Google search turns up is a cop in Texas once indicted for a road rage incident. Who knows if some unnamed adult beverage may have spawned it?

Tipping the Villa Mari scales at $55 is 'Ultima Thule', a blend of hoop-grown Syrah, Nebbiolo and Malbec. This is the highest price I have ever seen stamped on a Northern Michigan red table wine.

Doing some quick calculation, I concluded that with unlimited resources, Marty Lagina could install ProMelt radiant heating mats under the hoop houses for approximately $850,000 per acre. That way, if the bottom ever fell out of the wine market, he could grow orchids.

The question is not 'Is Ultima Thule worth it?', of course, because, like all things crafted and nurtured, wine is esoteric and loaded with intangibles—it is worth whatever someone is willing to pay for it. The question is, are you willing to support Marty Lagina's dream of growing Italian grapes in Northern Michigan by paying him $55 dollars a bottle when you can purchase a Marcarini Barolo Brunate 2006, which received 93 points from Robert Parker, for the same price?

That's the consumer decision which may decide the future of other hoop vineyards in the area, but my guess is that the market for $50+ bottles of Old Mission wine is limited. Not that there aren't ecological pluses to the *nellaserra* system; according to Lagina, fewer pesticides are needed and less work is required as hoop-grown vines tend to naturally short-crop, leading to higher quality clusters. And, walking the renewable walk, the entire operation is powered by two 7.5 KW windmills, making it a laudable achievement for that reason alone. Using unnatural components to alter a natural environment is a viticulture technique as old as irrigation systems.

But Lagina's statement that hoop houses simply seem like 'common sense' must leave a slightly bitter aftertaste among local vintners struggling to survive the savage season thrown their way. Common sense should be the domain of common man, and the idea that dodging nature is nothing more an oddly unexplored finger-snap in Northern Michigan is a little like Marie Antoinette saying about the breadless peasantry, *"Qu'ils mangent de la brioche"*—"Why don't they eat cake?"

How the commoners are supposed to find the dollars to make sense may wind up being the biggest mystery of all.

Ed O'Keefe:
The Overlord Of Old Mission

Ed O'Keefe may be the single most enthralling character in all of
Northern Michigan wine country, and guess what?

I can't tell you why.

That because, in our long conversations in a glassed-in porch
overlooking what is probably the most enthralling view in Northern

Michigan wine country, he told me that all the really riveting stuff was off the record. This includes the sort of source-names, confirmed places and dates and backup evidence to lend perfect journalistic credence to his tales of danger and intrigue as a narcotic agent for the US Treasury and his subsequent...

Well, there I go. I can't say.

What I can say is that Ed O'Keefe is a fireplug's fireplug—an indomitable Irish impresario who out-Cagneys Cagney. I can also point out that the publishable highlights of his life story are nearly as fascinating as those that are not. He was born in southwest Philadelphia in 1934—a time when Irish and Italian mobs were at each other's throats over control of the city's prostitution, extortion, labor racketeering and narcotics trade. From a tightly knit Irish-American clan that valued integrity, honesty, and above all, perseverance, it's no wonder he wound up firmly on the sunny side of the law.

"Find something you're good at and stick with it," Ed O'Keefe remembers. "That's what my Dad told me; that's the key to success."

Dad may or may not have realized that Ed would end up being a success at nearly everything he turned his hand to, which makes for a lively interview, but also, a very convoluted and hectic résumé. At John Bartram Senior High, he lettered in every sport and excelled at diving; at West Chester University tumbling skill earned him a spot on the National Gymnastics Team and he made first-cut in the 1952 US Olympics. Somehow, during his spare time in the midst of all this he managed to enlist in the military and serve as Captain in the Airborne Special Forces in Europe—remaining a Reserve Officer until the late '80s. Among his more jaw-dropping of accomplishments during this period of his life was the perfect score O'Keefe received on the Army fitness test, making him (at the time) one of only three people in US history ever to do so.

Law school followed the war; he left only when an opportunity to sign on with the US Treasury Department arose. In 1957, O'Keefe began to work as an undercover narcotics agent in New York City—at a time when Harry F. Anslinger, Federal Narcotics Commissioner, told a Senate Judiciary subcommittee, "If you had the Army, the Navy, the Coast Guard, the F.B.I., the Customs Service and our narcotics service, you would not stop heroin from coming through the Port of New York."

This is where the interview sort of derailed; the tonnage of tales about the dangerous life he led during the late years of the Fifties, rubbing shoulders with the underworld, occupied the rest of the afternoon; some of the wheels and deals made by his end of the agency have repercussions lasting to this day.

None have much to do with wine, however, so we can fast-forward to 1974. By that time, O'Keefe had proven himself as adept as a businessman as he had at everything else, and had opened a string of extended-care health nursing homes in the Midwest. Headquartered in Southfield, he built a summer home in Acme, Michigan, just east of Traverse City. The business was doing phenomenally well, and as any tax man worth his salt will tell you, if you're looking to diversify your holdings with a shelter where you will more than likely lose money, wineries are a pretty safe bet.

Three things you could bank on with an Ed O'Keefe wine venture: First, he was going to do it his way; second, he was going to do it the right way, and third, if he lost money, it wouldn't be for long. All three

161

proved accurate, and Chateau Grand Traverse has become the largest and most diverse winery in Northern Michigan; one of only a handful of Michigan wineries with a presence that reaches beyond state borders.

One reason is size—most wineries here produce enough wine to keep their tasting rooms and a few local restaurants supplied; that's it. At a hundred thousand cases per year, Chateau Grand Traverse can export, and has found customers in Europe and China.

The other, and undoubtedly more important reason for CGT's wider reach is its mass-market appeal. From the outset, Ed O'Keefe insisted on going where no commercial Michigan operation had dared to go before: *Vitis vinifera,* a.k.a. European grape varieties, which in 1974, nobody—not the locals, not the old timers, not the the horticulture department at Michigan State University—thought could survive here.

In fact, the venture was quietly referred to as *'O'Keefe's Folly'.* According to Craig Cunningham of Vine Care Inc., a vineyard management company, "At the time, commonly accepted data suggested if the temperature falls below -9°F, the most fruitful primary buds of vinifera varietals are almost entirely wiped out."

Of course, what the professional farmers and amateur meteorologists left out of their formula was Ed O'Keefe, who enlisted an unlikely ally: The 'Johnny Appleseed of Riesling', Dr. Helmut Becker, who came from Geisenheim Oeologogical and Viticutural school in Germany to assess the situation. Together they concluded that with a little work, Old Mission (rather than the slightly cooler Leelanau Peninsula) could sustain cold-hardy riesling.

That 'little work' wound up being the job of moving a million cubic yards of soil to produce a south-facing slope which would receive maximum sunlight while benefitting from the higher elevation and moderating effect of Grand Traverse Bay. O'Keefe planted 27 acres of Riesling, 17 acres of Chardonnay and one of Merlot, becoming the first large-scale grower of *vinifera* in the state.

Forty years later, the revolution begun by those 55 acres has raised Michigan's wine profile from joke to juggernaut, and I guarantee, if Ed O'Keefe started planting palm trees up and down M-37 in front of his tasting room, MSU would send horticultural students to write thesis papers and the neighbors wouldn't blink an eye.

At eighty-three, the chutzpah crown remains firmly on Ed O'Keefe's feisty Irish head; and, as my multi-hour, unpublishable interview made plain, his boundless wit and razor-sharp memory makes even stories about beating traffic tickets riveting—to me, anyway.

And at all events, the true story is in his wines, and he remains active in those decisions even while gradually turning over the everyday business reins to sons Ed Jr. and Sean.

But retire? I don't see that as an option and I have no doubt that Ed O'Keefe will be pouring Chateau Grand Traverse at God's retirement party.

LA BéCASSE: JUST BECAUSE

Spackling the United States are tiny, regional restaurants so fantastic that they are the only reason their associated towns are even listed on the map.

Maple City, near the fair banks of Glen Lake, is one such municipality. With a population of 207, *Michigan TripAdvisor* lists—somewhat optimistically—'2 Things To Do in Maple City!'.

The other one is a resale shop.

And according to chef/owner Guillaume Hazaël-Massieux, La Bécasse is actually not even *in* Maple City—it's in Burdickville, a community so tiny that its population figure cannot be found in any atlas. I can vouch for at least three: Chef Guillaume, his wife Brooke and their daughter Margot; the rest is up to the Census Bureau.

How a graduate of L'Institut Paul Bocuse in Lyon who grew up in the West Indies and interned at Grand Rapids' five-star Grand Plaza Hotel wound up in a resident-free hamlet in Northern Michigan is a testimonial to the lure of Leelanau Peninsula. The fact that the restaurant remains open—and even crowded—throughout the hibernation months is a testimonial to the quality of La Bécasse.

"Ending up in this small corner of the world?" Hazaël-Massieux smiles through his lilting Parisian cadence. "You're right; it makes absolutely no sense. After I served my mandatory time in the military [teaching the culinary arts in the Caribbean], I sent out three hundred applications. Of the twenty or so responses I received, the Grand Plaza seemed the most promising."

From there, after a three-year stint as guest chef for Steelcase, he took over the kitchen at Toulouse in Saugatuck—another Michigan resort community with a reputation for its surprisingly sophisticated dining scene.

Chef Gillaume describes his ascension to Leelanau, putting the Bocuse in Bécasse, like this: "The restaurant was already quite legendary; Peachy and John Rentenbach had done such a marvelous job over eighteen years—it was always my goal to maintain the charm they'd established here while making the culinary aspects more in line with what the French people eat on a daily basis; we're a French country inn."

Admittedly, this may involve UPSing truffles from New York and FedExing fish from overseas, but for a restaurant of this quality, one of the pluses is the price structure, high-end among local bars and grills perhaps, but bargain for those with an appreciation for culinary brilliance. Risotto with Michigan morels and roasted local squash is a vegetarian's Valhalla; grilled hanger steak in truffle sauce transports any carnivore to the Happy Hunting Ground.

"I want to earn enough to live, of course," Chef Gillaume declares of his menu pricing, "but I'm not here to rip anyone off. I was at a bistro in Manhattan selling roasted chicken for $80. It's insane."

His wine list shows similar sense; La Bécasse is a winner of Wine Spectator's 'Award of Excellence' for a selection that leans heavily toward French classics and includes numerous Michigan gems; prices run from $30 to $600, with the bulk of the offerings entrenched toward the scale's lower end.

Hazaël-Massieux has his sommelier's certificate, and of the products of his adopted peninsula he says, with all the candor I've come to expect, "Some of the reds have a way to go; they are pricey in comparison to what they offer. Except for Gamay—Chateau Grand Traverse makes a beautiful wine from this grape, and I am a huge fan of Beaujolais. For a domestic sparkling wine, a Pinot Gris or a Riesling, it wouldn't occur to me to go anywhere else for my wine list. Not Oregon, not Washington; there's no need. What we are doing right here in Northern Michigan is better than any of them."

Mike Jacobson's Long Distance Romance

In most *affaires de cœur*, long-distance romance rarely works out for the best, but in the case of Mike Jacobson and Leelanau Cellars, it's proven to be a match made in heaven.

A lawyer and businessman from Grand Rapids, Jacobson bought a three hundred acre parcel of Leelanau farmland in the late 1960s and contracted a scion of one of the oldest local farm families to manage it. Chuck Kalchik was Leelanau to the bone, having lived elsewhere only once in his life—when he served in the armed forces.

When discussing Northern Michigan wine country, and the roots of the revolution—grapes—a lot of names are tossed around: Rink, O'Keefe, Mawby, etc. But Jacobson and Kalchik, not as often. And that's probably a shame, because they were among the groundbreakers who saw the future through wine-colored glasses, and were ballsy enough aside the ones that they'd previously worn—Kalchik especially—which were cherry red.

"You look around the industry now, the wine country, and it looks pretty lovely," Mike reminisces. "But it's been a long road—as tough as it has been exciting."

Team Jacobson/Kalchik's move from cherry orchard to vineyard began in 1974, when they planted twenty acres of hybrids, varieties that were under experiment by a handful of contemporary visionaries. That included Aurora, Baco Noir, De Chaunac and Vignoles, vinified under the imported skill set of UC Davis Graduate and St. Julian alum Nick Stackhouse—another linchpin name in Leelanau's vinography.

"We made two key purchases: One was an old cherry processing plant we picked up from Chuck's uncle and converted to a winery, and the other was an old barn along M-37 where we opened one of Traverse City's first tasting rooms. We produced a white, a red, a rosé and a spice wine—the wine that has since evolved into Witches Brew.'

The winery rambled along a fairly straight path for a couple of years; Jacobson was content with the basic, reliable hybrids. But the evolving tastes of wine drinkers in that era, along with some personal and directional soul-searching, led to a re-envisioned Leelanau Cellars. In 1987, Bill Skolnik was brought on board to help, in part, devise a new business model with a view toward a sustainable future. That involved a new, contemporary label, a set of proprietary blends and a focus less on hybrids and more on the *vinifera* vines which had, by then, proven able to withstand Leelanau winters.

He planted Chardonnay in a new vineyard on Tatch Road, just south of Omena, laying the agricultural foundation for what today is his flagship wine, 'Tall Ship'. Meanwhile, he was able to dovetail an upgraded wine package with a growing acceptance among marketers to Michigan wine; Meijer was one of the first wider-audience retail outlets to hop on board.

That, in part, was responsible for a growth spurt that took Leelanau Cellars through the nineties and beyond; it is, today, based on tax records (one of the few reliable ways to gauge a winery's size) the largest winery in Michigan—even larger than St. Julian, mid-Michigan's powerhouse.

And the most remarkable part is that, other than weekends and forays north during the summer, Jacobson has largely directed the play from afar. His son Bob has worked various jobs at the winery over the years (beginning, Mike explains, the summer that an internship in Washington DC fell through), stamping a hands-on Jacobson signet to the operation, but as for himself, Mike says, "I've never lived up in Leelanau. I've always managed to hire people who understood the vision and brought with them their own sense of place and their own tool kit."

Among the series of influential winemakers who followed Skolnik, Shannon Walters figures highly in Jacobson's estimation: "He was instrumental in some of the marketing decisions that led to our largest period of growth. Awards of which we are still proud, like making the list of '30 Best Merlots in America' in *Wine & Spirits* magazine for our 2005 Merlot, happened during his tenure."

Walters left to help start 45 North, and Jacobson brought in an interesting choice to be his replacement: Nichole Birdsall, from the ground-zero of American winemaking, Healdsburg, California. She brought with her a pedigree in bulk production at Korbel and organic production at Bonterra, providing invaluable stabilizing technique for larger scale production.

Now, in Nichole's wake, it is David Hill and consultant Chas Catherman who are poised to point the winery's compass toward the future. This will involve a focused attention to the best of the hybrids, potentially some newer ones under current development as well as renewed commitment to vinifera which can produce consistently and well in the microclimate—and Chardonnay leads the pack.

Meanwhile Bob Jacobson, now president of the operation oversees all, while Mike remains comfortably ensconced in Grand Rapids.

Over the years, I've met plenty of lawyers who wanted to be winery owners, plenty of winery owners who wanted to be winemakers, plenty of winemakers who wanted to be winery owners—and if that failed, folks who wanted to go back and finish law school. But Mike Jacobson—now 78—has figured out away to fill in all the blanks from afar and thus, perhaps, has found the best of all possible worlds.

Lee Lutes: Putting the 'Star' in Black Star

You don't need a degree in finance to know a gold mine when you see it, but Lee Lutes has one anyway. And by gold mine, I don't mean cash flow that cascades at the expense of ideology, but a brass ring grab in the heart of wine country where a vintage can be as big a disaster as it can be a godsend—and coming up with the prize.

If there can be a 'perfect storm' in nature, perhaps there can be a 'perfect convergence' in human nature, which seems to be case when Lutes was approached by Don Coe and Kerm Campbell to become a managing partner in Black Star Farms. Coe had the class, the pockets and sauce savvy—he was once the president of Hiram Walker—while Campbell's rap sheet included being the CEO of The Prince Group and the president of Herman Miller; but as a grape grower, he also had good old Michigan dirt beneath his fingernails. In 1997, they had purchased a sprawling, 120-acre horse farm on Leelanau's east coast and laid the groundwork for a stellar winery in the center of an appellation that was just beginning to find its stride. Key to success was engaging the right winemaking partner, and in Lee Lutes all the stars seemed to have aligned.

Lee was a local kid then at Peninsula Cellars; a winemaker who understood the value of hybrids as well as the nuances of blends, but— having lived in Australia and trained in Italy—he also had a deep and abiding love for *vinifera,* especially red wine grapes.

"My fondest earliest memories are filled with Australian Riesling," he says; "sitting outside in a vineyard in Yalumba, my folks sipping wine with friends while I marveled at the beauty of the surroundings. That image has stayed with me throughout my life, and possibly, directed it."

His folks had moved to Sydney, then Adelaide, to pursue teaching opportunities, ultimately moving back to the United States and settling in Traverse City for the same reason. By then, Lee was ten, and spent his teen years in Northern Michigan, waiting tables and banking proceeds to pursue that finance degree at MSU. "I went to work for E.F. Hutton directly out of college, but I never forgot those beautiful Australian afternoons. By the time of the 1987 crash, I'd learned enough about brokerage to realize that the guy I was working for was a crook, so, like my parents did, I hauled off and moved back to Australia.

I spent the next few months doing a grand walkabout, meeting viticultural types and hanging out in vineyards."

But love beckoned, and within a year he was back, following his girlfriend (now wife) Terry to New York where she was a student. After a brief stint with importer Neil Rosenthal—quickly concluding that peddling wine on the streets of Manhattan was not a career for a 23-year-old noob from the Midwest—he went to work at Union Square Café, then among the top wine restaurants in the world. Danny Meyer taught him retail lessons that he retains today; meanwhile he was able to pick up some cellar-rat hours at Long Island's Gristina Vineyards. At the time, Gristina's winemaker was Larry Perrine—now at Channing Daughters—and Lee credits his mentorship for having helped train his superb wine palate.

During a tour of Europe, culminating in five days at VinItaly, he met winemaker Elisabetta Currado, whose father was a Piemontese pioneer, among the first bottle wines with a single vineyard designation. She took on Lee as 'her jolly' (his term) which has no 'pool boy' connotations; (Terry was there) but what she called her assistant.

Like Australia, his memories of the Italian wine country are steeped in sunny nostalgia: "Nobody could replicate that kind experience," he says. "It was my stroke of luck to end up in Castiglione Falletto, with room and board supplied and a stipend to boot. $300 a month wasn't a lot, but nobody starves in Italy. I learned about lesser know DOCs like Dolcetto di Ovada, and varietals like Arneis, at which the Currados excelled."

In 1992, Northern Italy suffered one of the wettest vintages in viticultural history, with Biblical-quality rains at harvest. He and Terry returned to Traverse City, only to find one of the wettest vintages in viticultural history, déjà vu all over again. Fortunately, he was hired by Bill Skolnik at Peninsula Cellars and dove into the Michigan wine scene headfirst, blown away by the ability of local grower Warren Raftshol to succeed with European grapes in Leelanau: "Raftshol Red [a field blend done at Peninsula Cellars] was the first wine I can recall that gave people a solid idea of what vinifera could do up here. I was as impressed as everybody else."

Fast forward to 1998, when it was Don Coe and Kerm Campbell's turn to be impressed—and the feeling was mutual. In them, he found partners with a wine vision directed by quality and stoked with a significant investment. An invaluable part of the Black Star business plan was adopting a co-op mentality, where a number of wine grape growers would have a financial interest in the company and—the theory went—have a bigger stake in growing quality fruit. Says Lee, "The idea was unique for Leelanau, but it was a sound principal: If you can give me fruit good enough to make a twenty dollar bottle of wine instead of a fifteen dollar bottle of wine, everybody benefits. Don and Kerm own 63% of the business; the rest is divided up between growers and myself. No decision is made without the core group's approval."

Success of the plan seems most obvious in the fact that although Black Star Farms is by no means the biggest wine producer in the appellation, it is arguably the most diverse and among the most talked about. Here, there is a premium placed on innovation (the short-lived, on-site cheese-making operation, for one) and evolution is constant. It is rare to wander into one the three tasting rooms and not find something new, eclectic and frequently puzzling: Distilled mead is an example.

Coe's Hiram Walker tenure made him the head cheerleader for an on-premise distillery, and—with Lutes as the distiller—has seen the release of a number of beautifully precise, award-devouring *eaux de vie* (fruit brandies) from nearly all from the locally-grown standards; cherries, apples, apricots. Distilled mead is a new one; part of the diversified face that Black Star Farms likes to put on its 'argritainment' variety show, making customers eager to find out what's making a premier performance on any given visit.

As for the future, Lee Lutes—with a perfectly straight face—points to a couple of grape cultivars that should have most wine people raising their eyebrows: Marquette and Gamay.

Gamay is the bellwether grape of Beaujolais, but it has struggled to make a statement in most other wine regions. In the Loire Valley, it is often blended with Cabernet Franc, although in Ontario's Niagara Peninsula, as a stand-alone, it has reached heights that some consider on par with Cru Beaujolais. In Northern Michigan, Chateau Grand Traverse's Gamay Noir has been a light, tart, plum-flavored winner for decades, but few other local producers have relied on it. Lee Lutes has five acres planted and plans for more: He loves it for its versatility as well as its fidelity.

"In warm vintages, I have no doubt that we can produce serious Gamay. It's a prolific grape, tough through the winter, and even in years where it doesn't entirely ripen it doesn't produce green or vegetative flavors. And in wet years, its relatively thick skins can withstand a lot of abuse. With Pinot Noir, thin skin and cluster compactness turn it into a gerbil-on-the-vine [mushy and virtually impossible to work with].

Gamay is durable—the integrity of the fruit holds together beautifully after rain."

And then there's Marquette. Marquette is a fairly new hybrid, introduced by the University of Minnesota in 2006; it's related to both Frontenac and Pinot Noir and is not only extremely cold hardy and disease resistent, but unlike most red wine hybrids, it has a strong *vinifera* profile, similar in flavor (blackberry, cherry, black pepper) to Malbec. And it ripens consistently in northern climates, with high sugar and moderate acidity.

"As a blending grape, Marquette will be viticultural gold. To produce reliable red wines every vintage in Northern Michigan it makes no sense to rely entirely on *vinifera*; the yield for the classic reds in 2014 is abysmal. And if my decades up here have shown me anything about weather patterns, winters like the last one come in cycles, sometimes four years in a row. We need to grow a backbone of red grapes that will ripen regardless of the season; Marquette is impervious to most temperatures we can throw at it; supposedly, to minus thirty. Time will tell.

He concludes: "But that is the amazing part of being a winemaker on the frontier of the arctic—we adapt. The negative side, of course, is that every vintage is a question mark. The positive side, the one I love, is that the dynamics are always alive, always a new challenge to tackle."

CORNEL OLIVIER

THE SOUTH AFRICAN CONNECTION

It's hard to imagine a place farther from the balmy vineyards of South Africa than the shivery snowscapes of Old Mission Peninsula, and it's just as hard to find a wine contrast as striking as the intense, juicy-fruit Cabernets of the Cape to the steely Rieslings of Northern Michigan.

So it has never failed to intrigue me that fully 25% of Old Mission's winemakers are South African.

Of course, lest that number seem more intriguing than it actually is, there are only eight wineries on Old Mission Peninsula, so that means that two of the winemakers are from South Africa—Cornel Olivier at Two Lads Winery and Coenraad Stassen at Brÿs Estate Vineyard & Winery.

I sat with Cornel in the 2 Lads tasting room—a polished steel-and-glass gem with a vast view of the East Bay—and heard the tale of his cross-hemisphere eno-journey from WO to AVA, heat to sleet, Rust en Vrede to rust on pickup truck, a decade and a half ago.

"I come from a huge agricultural community in Stellenbosch, probably the most important red wine region in Africa. I grew up around agriculture and that's all I wanted to do. But, during Apartheid sanctions, we were limited in terms of our exposure to wines from outside the country. I loved the red wine of Stellenbosch, but it wasn't until 1998, my last year of school [the prestigious Elsenburg Agricultural College] that I first tasted a Sonoma Zinfandel and was amazed."

He credits that experience to his mentor, the late Louw Engelbrecht, former winemaker at Zonnebloem, Blauberg and Durbanville Hills, and it was a serendipitous introduction indeed: "Before that," he says, "I had my mind set on an apprenticeship in Europe; that's the place where most of Elsenburg graduates were going. But that Zinfandel—it was exactly the kind of big, robust, dry red that I wanted to make."

With sinewy arms folded over a black North Face windbreaker, Cornel Olivier is as big and robust as his pet wines—you glance at him, listen to his thick South African rumble, note the confidence in his carriage, and you tend to think 'professional rugby player' before you think 'sparkling wine maker'.

And he's also nearly as dry as his 2012 Cabernet Franc; the only grin that crossed his face during the hour I spoke to him was when I asked him to spell some of the multi-syllabic, Dutch-sounding words with which he seasons his speech—he may have paid better attention during primary fermentation class than during spelling. Whatever the reason, the rare Olivier smile is like a beam of sunshine across the broad, leaden Bay outside the tasting room window.

Back again to the corrugated steel and poured concrete showroom, the flagship architectural statement in the entire appellation: In 2010, *Food & Wine* described the sleek 2 Lads interior as being 'right out of the pages of *Dwell* magazine' while *The Compass* maintains that 'the contemporary room is unique among Michigan wineries, capturing the fresh perspective and boldness of the wines produced there.' Indeed, to reach the place, you have to pass through a sculpted iron gate and amble up a scenic hillside, feeling for all the world that you are visiting a stuff-strutting winery in Napa or Australia's Adelaide Hills. When you get into the meat and potatoes section, however, you may be as surprised as I was to learn that the 2 Lads' entire output is around 7000 cases a year. With an average bottle price of $25, and two lads drawing paychecks, the inescapable conclusion to be drawn within this magnificent milieu is that there is a third lad in the picture, and one with rather substantial pockets.

And that happens to be the father-in-law Chris Baldyga (Lad 2), who staked them in this wild and beautiful Northern Michigan venture.

Cornel tells the tale like this:

In 2006, while he was up to his neck in metaphorical alligators in the vineyards, the cellar and the tasting room at Brÿs Estate (as the winemaking South African who preceded the current Brÿs Estate winemaking South African), he ran into his old friend Chris Baldyga, then preparing to move to Australia to attend wine marketing school. In the course of the conversation, Baldyga asked him how much capital would be required to start an Old Mission winery—apparently, such a business model was Plan B in case the Australia thing didn't work out. According to Baldyga, he already had some investors interested. That last bit of news got Cornel's cerebral cogs churning, and he suggested that, if Baldyga were to head in that direction, they should consider teaming up; he'd make the wine while Chris handled the marketing end of the equation.

The details aren't entirely clear—maybe not even to those involved—but the upshot is that by the end of 2006, with dad-in-law's blessing, Baldyga and Olivier (henceforth and forever known as the 2 Lads), found an existing farm with 11 acres planted to grapes and another nine to cherries, which were immediately pushed out in favor of more grapes.

With those grapes, Cornel went on to craft a series of wines that have been received with no small amount of praise and wonder across Michigan's wine community and beyond. In a 2012 interview with *Awesome Michigan*, when asked how many of his wines won awards since the first vintage, Chris Baldyga responded, truthfully, "All of them."

The irony, of course, is that for a man who was intent on producing world-class red wine, Cornel Oliver has staked his primary claim in the heart of the white wine world, even excelling at a variety which he had previously shrugged at: Riesling. Having asked a number of Michigan eno-scholars who produces the best Northern Michigan Riesling, I found that 2 Lads was nearly always mentioned among the top three, even though they only have a single acre of Riesling planted

"I didn't even begin to dial in Riesling until 2010, when Sean O'Keefe (Chateau Grand Traverse) convinced me to attend the 2010 Riesling Rendezvous in Washington. I was impressed with Austrian Riesling especially, but at the luncheon where Michigan Riesling was served exclusively, I was converted. I bought 25 tons and did some experimenting, nine separate fermentations which I halted at various residual sugars. Chemistry is key to quality; for our climate, ideal seems to be a TA [total acidity] between seven and eight, a pH of around 3.28 and an RS [residual sugar] of 1.1%."

Riesling may or may not play a bigger role in the future of this lad, but sparkling wine most certainly will. Having bought the equipment to produce sparkling wine in house, 2 Lads in one of the few Northern Michigan wineries not dependant on Larry Mawby to put the sparkle in the still.

Just as certain is that Cornel's fingernails will continue to get dirty in Michigan vineyard soil—for all the passion he puts into production, agriculture is in his soul:

"I'm happiest in the vineyards, within the environment and the potential; that's where the power is, and being in the dirt is where I love it the most."

Cornel Olivier came to Northern Michigan via an exchange program at Ohio State University; his initial goal was to land a gig in California, where his beloved Zinfandel grew. But Bernd Croissant, winemaker at

Chateau Grand Traverse, happened to see his résumé and enticed him north to accept an internship. Despite leaving South Africa when temperatures were 92° and arriving in Traverse City when temperatures were 20°, he stuck it out and plans to keep sticking for the foreseeable future.

COENRAAD STASSEN

With Coenraad Stassen, who hails from a different part of South Africa entirely, the trajectory was eerily similar. Stassen, likewise rugby-rugged and eno-able, is from Ladysmith in KwaZulu-Natal—a focal point in Boer War history and a diverse wine region in South Africa's middle east. He also attended Elsenburg, now called the Cape Institute for Agricultural Training, but cut his winemaking teeth in-country, spending eight years in Klein Karoo, arguably the most diverse wine region in South Africa.

He obtained a degree in Senior Cellar Technology (whatever that is), and, like his countryman Olivier, he came to Old Mission via Ohio State's exchange program. He was hired at Chateau Chantal, whose faux-château is as big a visual as 2 Lads' modernistic sleek-a-torium.

You see these kind of crown-jewel strongholds in Old Mission Peninsula far more often than you do in neighboring Leelanau Peninsula; that's in part because an acre of Old Mission turf may cost twice as much as an acre of land in Leelanau. Old Mission has less surface area to work with, and to many wealthy retirees, it is an arctic Arcadia. It is downstate accessible to the kids, with upscale accessories like championship golf and Caribbean-blue bay views. As a result, on the auction block, retirement homes often go head-to-head with vineyard spaces and in the subsequent bidding wars, when land prices rise to a point that is beyond what a Michigan winery can possibly recoup, The Golden Parachute Club wins.

If the rising cost of dirt becomes such that a winery can't afford to expand, is that a bad thing? Not necessarily, according to Coenraad Stassen, who has, in his own charismatic struggle, managed to raise the bar to some breathtaking heights by making the most out of the fruit grown on existing acreage.

In 2007, in Cornel's wake in 2007, he moved from Chantal to Brÿs Estate. The South African connection is simply coincidence, more so when the two—who did not know each other in South Africa—found that they had cousins who were friends and numerous acquaintances in common. If there is a similar vigor and precision to their winemaking, it is likely due to the quality of their education.

At Brÿs, Stassen has focused entirely on estate grown vinifera, has brought home more than 250 medals in national and international wine competitions. Nothing to sniff at, but you know what? The judges do anyway.

Is he currently the best winemaker on the Old Mission Peninsula? That's not a stake I'm willing to put in the ground, because (alas) I have not sampled every wine from every Old Mission winery. But, have I ever tasted a more consistent portfolio in the peninsula? I haven't.

That said—and as has been said—growing with the vineyard does not always mean 'growing the vineyard', and neither he nor the Brÿs bunch (son and daughters are involved) have any wish to move far past the 8500 cases of wine they currently produce annually. Figuring that an acre of OMP land may sell for $45,000 or more, with an additional $15,000 needed for vineyard planting and subsequent management, and three years minimum before the first, often mediocre harvest hits the crusher, at 3 tons per acre making about 400 cases, each bottle will cost wannabe winery wankers more than $20—sometimes a lot more. Unfortunately, in 2013, there is only so much a bottle of Michigan wine can command and the average price of a Brÿs wine is around $23.

So with the ancient wisdom of The Five Sangomas of KwaZulu-Natal, Stassen aims at quality over quantity, content with what he has to work with and leaving that extra pricey acre of Old Mission terroir to the Metamucil crowd.

BILL SKOLNIK: FINDING A FINGER IN THE MITTEN

When somebody uses the word 'love' and 'hate' with equal pith, equal conviction and equal authority in the same exhale, you know you're in for an interesting conversation.

Which is why I tracked Bill Skolnik down in the first place, but more on that in a sec.

Skolnik hasn't made a drop of Northern Michigan wine in over a decade, but he is as integral to the story as any Jacobson, any O'Keefe, any Rink. He is, in fact, a *bamf* ex-Marine with a burly red beard and a leatherneck grip who stormed ashore in Traverse City like it was Tripoli, arriving to attend the Great Lakes Maritime Academy and staying to steer a couple of local winemakers out of the viniferous doldrums. To his credit, he'd brought along a sea bag of experience he'd picked up as a cellar rat at Long Island's Pindar Vineyards.

For those of you who don't know about Long Island's North Fork— Skolnik's original stomping ground, whose accent *(Lawn GY-luhnd)* he retains, thickly—it's sort of like Manhattan's *Green Acres*, where city folks looking to escape urban sprawl and the nearby Hamptons find themselves experiencing culture shock amid the smell of barnyard animals and pesticides. Like Northern Michigan, it's also one of the country's clandestine hotspots for cool weather wine grapes, and similarly, has enjoyed a quality renaissance over the past couple of decades. Pindar Vineyards was a leader in that frontal assault, using modern winemaking theory and canny vineyard management techniques. Possessed of a brain that can absorb knowledge like a squeegee, Skolnik used his boot-camp time at Pindar to pick up a lot of the tips that he'd later transplant to Michigan.

Why Michigan? For starters, other than having been accepted at the Maritime Academy, then as now, he can't stand Long Island.

I ran into Skolnik in the rustic, birch-and-pine grill he manages on the shores of Lake Michigan in Glen Arbor, and frankly, I was surprised he'd agreed to meet. If ever a wine country character's reputation preceded him, it was Bill's; he's spoken of with a certain amount of head-shaking reverence in Northern Michigan, as much by those who worked for him as those he worked for. In fact, since he's been out of the winemaking business since 2001, he seemed suspicious at worst and puzzled at best that I'd want to include a chapter on him. The only analogy that made sense was this: For the same reason that NFL Today hires ex-football players like Boomer Esiason to provide color commentary, background information on the players, strategy analysis and injury reports—not to mention the odd chuckle.

Fair to say that Skolnik provided plenty of commentary, both color and off-color, some of which is not suitable for a family wine book, but all of which proved that his position among the founding fathers of the region's character-study is firmly entrenched.

Take his memories of Ed O'Keefe (another one of this narratives larger-than-life, won't-suffer-fools-gladly curmudgeons):

The two of them were coming back from a sales sortie in Sault St. Marie one blizzardy evening, a couple of red pops over the line, when Bill—at the wheel—was pulled over by a state trooper. He claims that O'Keefe leaned over to the cop and said, "Arrest my friend; he just robbed a bank." And Bill, privately praying to the patron saint of one-too-many that he wouldn't be breathalyzed, replied: "See, Officer? That's why *I'm* the one driving."

No harm, no foul; the cop let them go, and a couple of miles down the highway, Bill steered the car onto an off-ramp and settled the thing like a gentleman: By hauling O'Keefe out of the passenger seat and playing fisticuffs in the snowdrifts.

By all accounts, it was a draw. And, like a couple of men, it proved to be nothing more than a myoclonic jerk in the diaphragm of friendship, and soon afterward, O'Keefe gave Skolnik the official title of 'Intergalactic Sales Manager', claiming that he could sell red dirt to a Martian.

By his own admission, the former Marine admits he learned a boatload from the former Special Ops winery owner; they met by chance when Skolnik's buddy started dating Colleen O'Keefe, Ed's daughter. This was 1980, when interest rates were nudging 22% and the Great Lakes shipping industry was imploding; activity was reduced from 120 ships on the water to around 40. It seemed time, Bill notes, for a rakehell turn in his career plans.

Via Colleen O'Keefe, Skolnik had become enamored of Chateau Grand Traverse wine dogma and, having left the Academy, he hit up Ed O'Keefe for a job. Ed nibbled, but didn't bite, claiming he didn't have the cash flow for a new hiree. Skolnik proposed a plan—a Northern Michigan wine festival—to help fill the coffers, and, according to him, the subsequent Oktoberfest based on Riesling rather than beer did the trick; he says that O'Keefe was able to bank ten grand.

Now on board, Skolnik began to work alongside winemaker Mark Johnson, who'd graduated from the Geisenheim Grape Breeding Institute. His learning curve was broad, he says; he became embedded in Northern Michigan wine culture—from sales to vineyard management to winemaking.

As much as he reaped with O'Keefe, so—as confirmed by Mark Jacobson himself—did he sow in the peninsula to his immediate left. Lured to Leelanau Cellars to guide the operation through stormy seas during a series of disastrous vintages and a winemaker who apparently

189

spent more time inside his barrels than tending them, Skolnik advised Jacobson to sell the winery's useless and unbottled product to Fleischmann's Vinegar for a nickel a gallon and start over. It was a pill even more unpalatable than the last batch of wine, but Jacobson wisely gulped it down, and Skolnik made some quick adjustments in the next vintage, de-acidifying the wines and using a lab to analyze the fruit. He'd already come to understand the value in blends—hybrids, the cornerstone of consistency in the appellation, can make proprietary wines that don't wear consumer-confusing varietal names like Baco Noir or Vignoles; seasonal wines like Winter White can contain an array of grapes and *vinifera* can be combined in unusual, iconoclastic configurations (Gamay, Cabernet Franc, Merlot, Cabernet Sauvignon and Pinot Noir make up 'Vis a Vis') without tipping the canoe. Of equal importance, Skolnik helped hauled the brand into the modern era, hiring graphic designer Tim Nielsen to come up with a more user-friendly label.

But in the end, Skolnik insists, it was Meijer who saved the bacon. And for that glory, he shares the crown:

"A new marketing mindset helped, but Ed Baur, who was then the sales manager at Wicksall Distributors in Traverse City, believed in Michigan wine, and worked to assure that it got prominent shelf placement at the big stores. He was also key to our survival through rough financial spells, buying a hundred cases here, a hundred there, when he really didn't need them. His commitment to the program was instrumental in keeping the ship afloat."

By that point, Skolnik was already begin to sour on the wine business. He'd entered it at a time when, he says, "Your word was your bond—

deals were made with a handshake and the wine community in the United States was such a brotherhood that I could pretty much pick up a Napa phonebook, make a cold call to a random winemaker and have a two hour conversation about a certain technique."

By the late nineties, with the the burgeoning industry becoming more cutthroat, he returned to Long Island and overhauled some barnacled winery keels—notably at Osprey's Dominion, then struggling with a half-assed winemaker (the owner's nephew) and a crew of vineyard workers who would rather drink vodka than prune. Although everything Bill says has to be divided by the appropriate hyperbolic integer, he insists, "I transformed the place from an abused shithole to a winery worthy of a spread in any international wine magazine."

Then why the return to Northern Michigan, to take a substantial pay cut, retracing a worn path to Leelanau Cellars in 1999? Especially when that tenure only lasted a couple of years, and here he remains?

This is where Skolnik's hyperbole ends and his passion begins; here is where the *primum mobile* of 'love' and 'hate' that seem to swirl near his surface waters are most candid:

"I hate Long Island. Too crowded. In fact, I hate people; I really do. When I was back in New York, I was homesick even though I was home. I missed Northern Michigan every single day and wished I'd never left. I realized that I was in love with her."

Being a people, I have no doubt which side of emotional equation I fall into, but it is an undisputable fact is that the offense one feels at being flipped off is in direct proportion to the man behind the digit.

And although he hasn't made wine in more than a decade, Bill Skolnik's middle finger—along with his other nine digits—have left a couple of indelible handprints on Northern Michigan wine country.

DEPARTURES

The problem with Sleeping Beauty—as with all fairy tales—is that it leaves you with, *'And they lived happily ever after...'*

Even as a kid, you knew that in a world of witches and giants and polar vortices, the likelihood of that actually happening was slim.

Behind the gnarled strip malls and off-putting tourist traps that you'll need to dispatch before you can get to Northern Michigan wine country, you will find—as I did—a wealth of beauties, some sleeping like the great perched dunes that pile along the western shoreline, some alive and active like a harvest crew at work at daybreak in a sprawling acre of autumn Riesling. All are in the throes of seasonal transition; the sand shifts and slithers at a pace of about three feet per year while the wines of Leelanau and Old Mission wage an equally slow battle to win position on the world's wine stage.

There is no 'happily ever after' in these endless wars; there is only the pace of progress. Should another savage January descend upon Northern Michigan and lead to another systems failure, many of the most precious stops along the current Wine Trail—the mom 'n' pop ops clinging to life by the narrowest of margins—may find themselves unable to go another round. The relative behemoths, fighting in a higher weight class with the advantage of deeper pockets, will absorb their customers without question, perhaps by selling them wine that is pumped with sugar or enriched with juice from another time zone entirely. (One local winemaker who asked not to be mentioned by name made the declaration: "A lot of us put on a Mitten t-shirt, but in lousy harvests, we all end up wading through the same puddle of California juice.") But this is the face of a lifestyle; likewise, in a dozen millennia, Sleeping Bear Dunes may engulf downtown Traverse City.

The previous pages have been a state-of-the-art selfie, a scenic turnoff from which to admire Northern Michigan's wine presence as it was during a brief and early moment in a long, labyrinthian lifetime, moving inexorably toward a future which may or may not be entirely happy, when, in either case, this book will be nothing more than a dusty once-upon-a-time.

Made in the USA
Middletown, DE
06 April 2015